TOP-RATED
EVERGREEN
SHRUBS
AND HOW TO USE THEM IN YOUR GARDEN

This book was produced for Western Publishing Company, Inc., by the staff of Horticultural Associates, Inc., in cooperation with Amfac® Garden Products.

Executive Producer: Richard Ray
Contributing Authors: John Ford, Robert L. Ticknor
Consultants: Claire Barrett, Fred Galle, Ralph Miller, Carl A. Totemeier, Richard Turner, Joseph A. Witt
Photography: Michael Landis
Art Director: Richard Baker
Book Design: Judith Hemmerich
Associate Editors: Michael MacCaskey, Lance Walheim
Research Editor: Randy Peterson
Copy Editors: Greg Boucher, Miriam Boucher
Production Editor: Kathleen Parker
Book Production: Lingke Moeis
Illustrations: Charles Hoeppner, Roy Jones
Typography: Linda Encinas
Additional Photography: William Aplin
Cover Photo: Michael Landis
Acknowledgements: Bill Robinson, Japanese Garden Society of Oregon; Nancy Davidson Short, Seattle, WA; Van Winden's Nursery, Napa, CA; Whitings Nursery, St. Helena, CA.

For Western Publishing Company, Inc.:
Editorial Director: Jonathan P. Latimer
Senior Editor: Susan A. Roth
Copy Editor: Karen Stray Nolting

Golden Press • New York

Western Publishing Company, Inc.

Racine, Wisconsin

715.3
TOP

Top-Rated Evergreen Shrubs

This book is planned to help you select the best evergreen shrubs for a variety of uses around your home. The plants discussed in this book are widely available, dependable shrubs that were selected by gardeners, growers, and horticulturists as being top-rated plants.

What are evergreen shrubs? Plants that retain their foliage year-round are called evergreen. There are two kinds: needle-leaved evergreens, or conifers, which have narrow needlelike foliage, and broad-leaved evergreens, with flat, broadened foliage.

Plants with a full shape and many stems are usually called shrubs. Tall plants with a single trunk are called trees. However, some trees can be pruned into a shrublike form. Also, many trees have dwarf varieties that resemble shrubs. All plants described in this book can serve a shrub's purpose.

In the landscape: Evergreen shrubs have a variety of uses. Their year-round foliage is invaluable for concealing the foundation of a house and for creating privacy. Plant them as barrier hedges, to accent a walkway, or as a background for a flower bed.

Plant identification: The cross-reference list on page 63 matches the most widely used common names with the plant's botanical name, which is the primary identification used in this book.

Evergreen shrubs for your region: Climate is the most important factor influencing where a plant will grow successfully. The hardiness zones where each plant will give a top-rated performance are included with each plant entry. The charts on the following pages give additional information.

At left: Privets *(Ligustrum sp.)* are tough plants widely used for screens and hedges. Clusters of cream or white blossoms are borne on stem tips in summer.

Heavenly bamboo *(Nandina domestica)*

Glossy abelia *(Abelia x grandiflora)*

Burford holly *(Ilex cornuta)*

Mock orange *(Pittosporum sp.)*

3

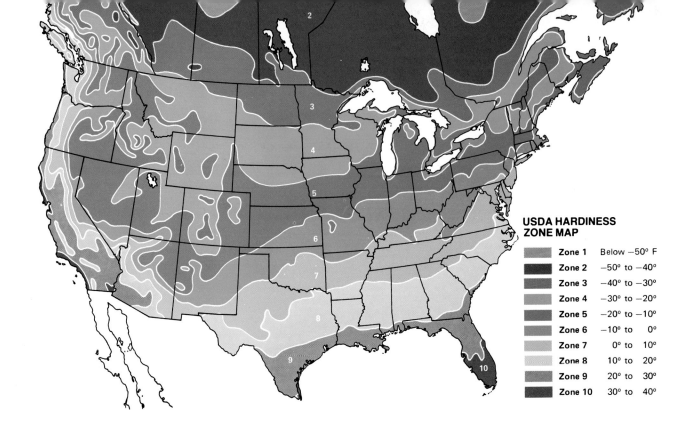

USDA HARDINESS ZONE MAP

Zone 1	Below −50° F
Zone 2	−50° to	−40°
Zone 3	−40° to	−30°
Zone 4	−30° to	−20°
Zone 5	−20° to	−10°
Zone 6	−10° to	0°
Zone 7	0° to	10°
Zone 8	10° to	20°
Zone 9	20° to	30°
Zone 10	30° to	40°

Climates for Evergreen Shrubs

The USDA plant hardiness map shows the average low temperatures throughout the United States and Southern Canada. It divides North America into 10 zones with the average minimum temperature of each zone differing by 10 degrees Fahrenheit. All plants in this book are labeled in the following charts and in the encyclopedia with the zones where their growth performance has been judged top-rated. Use the map to find your climate zone so you can select appropriate plants for your garden.

As every gardener learns, cold hardiness is only one factor of a plant's adaptation. A plant's ability to do well in a certain location depends on unique combinations of soil type, wind, rainfall, length and time of cold, humidity, summer temperatures, and temperatures in relation to humidity. For example, leucothoe requires slightly acid soil for healthy growth. Areas with high annual rainfall, such as the northeastern United States and the Pacific Northwest, have acid soil that is ideal for growing this plant.

In some other areas, though the climate might be acceptable for leucothoe, the soil is too alkaline. Peat moss or other acidifying soil amendments should be added to solve this problem.

The climates of California and Arizona are dramatically different from the rest of the United States. Summers are long and dry and frequent irrigation is necessary unless drought-resistant plants are selected. Native western plants such as wild lilac and coyote brush thrive under hot, dry climate conditions and are useful landscape plants for this region.

The USDA hardiness zone map does not take climate factors other than temperature into consideration. To give you additional information, the map on the opposite page divides the country into 10 climate regions. For a plant to be adapted to your area, it must be recommended both for your hardiness zone and your climate region. USDA Zones 8 to 10 are particularly complex in the western United States. Many plants that

cannot grow farther south than Zone 8 in the Deep South can grow in Zones 9 and 10 in the West. In these cases, it is best to follow regional recommendations.

The climates around your home:

Microclimates are the small climates around your home that differ slightly from the general climate of your area. The northern side of your property, which is probably partially shaded most of the day by your house, is a cold microclimate. The southern side of your home, which, unless shaded by trees, receives hot sun almost all day, is a warm microclimate. A good way to become aware of microclimates is by making a site plan.

Plants that are borderline hardy for your area may do well if you take protective measures such as providing wind or snow shelters and making use of your property's warm microclimates. Protected plants can often be grown successfully in the next colder zone.

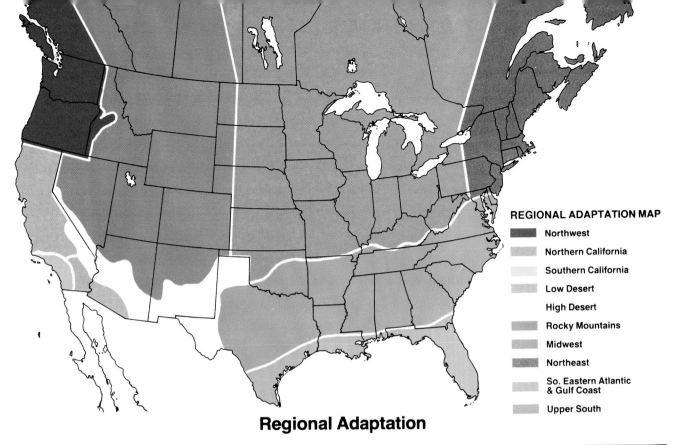

REGIONAL ADAPTATION MAP
- Northwest
- Northern California
- Southern California
- Low Desert
- High Desert
- Rocky Mountains
- Midwest
- Northeast
- So. Eastern Atlantic & Gulf Coast
- Upper South

Regional Adaptation

PLANT NAME	ZONES	NORTHWEST	NORTHERN CALIFORNIA	SOUTHERN CALIFORNIA	LOW DESERT	HIGH DESERT	ROCKY MOUNTAINS	MIDWEST	NORTHEAST	SO. EASTERN ATLANTIC & GULF COAST	UPPER SOUTH
Abelia x grandiflora	6-10	■	■	■	■	■		■	■	■	■
Azalea (See Rhododendron)											
Baccharis pilularis	8-10		■	■	■	■					
Berberis x gladwynensis 'William Penn'	5-8	■	■				■	■	■		■
Berberis julianae	6-8	■	■				■	■	■		■
Berberis x mentorensis	5-8	■	■				■	■	■		■
Buxus sp.	5-10	■	■				■	■	■	■	■
Callistemon sp.	8-10		■	■	■					■	■
Camellia sp.	7-10	■	■	■						■	■
Carissa grandiflora	10			■	■					■	
Ceanothus sp.	8-10	■	■	■							
Chamaecyparis obtusa	5-9	■	■					■	■		■
Chamaecyparis pisifera	5-9	■	■					■	■		■
Cistus x purpureus	8-10	■	■	■							
Cleyera japonica	8-10	■	■	■						■	■
Cocculus laurifolius	8-10		■	■	■						
Convolvulus cneorum	7-10		■	■	■					■	■
Coprosma repens	9-10		■								
Cotoneaster buxifolius	7-10	■	■	■	■				■	■	■
Cotoneaster congestus	6-10	■	■	■	■	■	■	■	■	■	■
Cotoneaster dammeri	5-10	■	■	■	■	■	■	■	■	■	■
Cotoneaster lacteus	7-10	■	■	■	■				■	■	■
Dodonaea viscosa	8-10		■	■	■						

Mugo pines *(Pinus mugo)* thrive in most regions, growing slowly into dense compact mounds.

Regional Adaptation

PLANT NAME	ZONES	NORTHWEST	NORTHERN CALIFORNIA	SOUTHERN CALIFORNIA	LOW DESERT	HIGH DESERT	ROCKY MOUNTAINS	MIDWEST	NORTHEAST	SO. EASTERN ATLANTIC & GULF COAST	UPPER SOUTH
Elaeagnus pungens	7-10	■	■	■	■				■	■	
Escallonia x exoniensis	7-10	■	■	■							
Euonymus fortunei	4-8	■	■					■	■		
Euonymus japonica	7-9	■	■		■	■				■	
Euonymus kiautschovica 'Manhattan'	6-9	■	■	■	■	■		■	■	■	
Fatsia japonica	8-10		■	■						■	
Gardenia jasminoides	8-10		■	■	■					■	
Grevillea 'Noell'	8-10		■	■	■						
Hebe sp.	9-10		■	■						■	
Hibiscus rosa-sinensis	9-10		■	■	■					■	
Ilex x altaclarensis 'Wilsonii'	6-10	■	■	■	■	■				■	
Ilex aquifolium	6-9	■	■	■					■	■	
Ilex cornuta	6-10	■	■	■			■	■	■	■	
Ilex crenata	5-10	■	■	■			■	■	■	■	
Ilex vomitoria	7-10		■	■	■					■	
Juniperus sp.	3-10	■	■	■	■	■	■	■	■	■	
Leucothoe axillaris	6-9	■	■					■	■		
Leucothoe fontanesiana	5-8	■	■					■	■		
Ligustrum japonicum	7-10	■	■	■	■	■			■	■	
Ligustrum lucidum	8-9	■	■	■	■	■				■	
Mahonia aquifolium	5-9	■	■	■	■	■	■	■	■	■	
Mahonia bealei	5-10	■	■	■	■	■	■	■	■	■	
Mahonia lomariifolia	8-10	■	■	■						■	
Murraya paniculata	9			■							
Myoporum laetum 'Carsonii'	8-10		■	■							

In spring, variegated tobira *(Pittosporum tobira* 'Variegata') bears creamy-white flowers scented like orange blossoms.

Regional Adaptation

PLANT NAME	ZONES	NORTHWEST	NORTHERN CALIFORNIA	SOUTHERN CALIFORNIA	LOW DESERT	HIGH DESERT	ROCKY MOUNTAINS	MIDWEST	NORTHEAST	SO. EASTERN ATLANTIC & GULF COAST	UPPER SOUTH
Myrtus communis	9-10		■	■	■	■					
Nandina domestica	6-10	■	■	■	■	■				■	■
Nerium oleander	8-10		■	■	■	■				■	■
Osmanthus heterophyllus	7-10	■	■	■						■	■
Photinia x fraseri	7-10	■	■	■	■	■				■	■
Picea sp.	2-8	■	■				■	■	■		■
Pieris sp.	5-9	■	■					■	■		■
Pinus sp.	2-8	■	■	■	■	■	■	■	■		■
Pittosporum tobira	8-10	■	■	■	■	■				■	■
Platycladus orientalis	6-10	■	■	■	■	■		■	■		■
Prunus caroliniana	7-10		■	■	■	■				■	■
Prunus laurocerasus	7-10	■	■					■	■	■	■
Pyracantha sp.	5-10	■	■	■	■	■	■	■	■		■
Raphiolepis indica	8-10	■	■	■	■	■				■	■
Rhododendron hybrids	4-10	■	■	■			■	■	■	■	■
Rosmarinus officinalis	7-10	■	■	■	■	■			■	■	■
Sarcococca hookerana humilis	7-10	■	■	■					■		■
Skimmia japonica	6-8	■	■						■		■
Taxus baccata	6-9	■	■	■				■	■		■
Taxus cuspidata	5-9		■					■	■		■
Taxus x media	5-9		■					■	■		■
Thuja occidentalis	3-9	■	■	■				■	■		■
Tsuga canadensis 'Pendula'	5-9	■	■					■	■		■
Viburnum odoratissimum	7-10	■	■	■						■	■
Viburnum suspensum	9-10		■	■						■	■
Viburnum tinus	7-10	■	■	■	■					■	■
Xylosma congestum	8-10		■	■	■	■				■	■

Using Evergreen Shrubs in Your Garden

Evergreen shrubs are the backbone of the landscape. During all four seasons they provide dependable greenery that dresses up your house and garden, providing a background for the seasonal changes of deciduous flowering shrubs and flowering annuals and perennials. The consistent appearance of evergreen shrubs is essential to combining the diverse elements in your landscape into a harmonious scene.

Besides being so crucial to the appearance of a yard and garden, evergreen shrubs fill many practical functions because their dense foliage serves to block both views and viewers year-round and to buffer strong winds. Both conifers (needle-leaved evergreens) and broad-leaved evergreens provide effective greenery for ornament and camouflage, though they have strikingly different appearances in the garden.

Conifers: Conifers are characterized by wax-covered leaves that are shaped like needles or scales. Sometimes called needle-leaved or narrow-leaved evergreens, conifers are a diverse group of plants that vary greatly in climate adaptation. Some, such as the junipers, are extremely tough plants that withstand drought, low winter temperatures, and poor soils. Their needlelike leaves evaporate little water even during periods of high temperatures. Others, such as spruce and Oriental arborvitae, are native to cool, moist areas with rich soils and only look their best under similar conditions.

When viewed from a distance, the narrow leaves of most conifers

At left: Evergreen shrubs visually blend your home and garden setting throughout the year, creating a backdrop for seasonal color.

Oregon grape *(Mahonia aquifolium)*

Oriental arborvitae *(Platycladus sp.)*

Red-tip photinia *(Photinia x fraseri)*

American arborvitae *(Thuja occidentalis)*

9

Contrast blue-green, gray-green, and dark green foliage to create elegant color effects.

Evergreen azaleas (Rhododendron hybrids), have handsome fine-textured foliage excellent in mass planting.

A low boxwood hedge (Buxus sp.) enhances shiny xylosma (Xylosma congestum) and Meyer lemon (Citrus sp.).

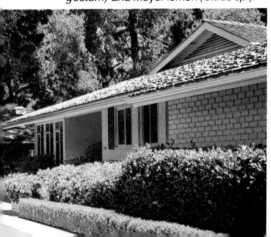

blend together into a pattern of thin lines that has a fine-textured appearance. The soft look of most conifers creates a serene feeling, which explains why conifers are frequently used in Oriental meditation gardens.

Many needle-leaved shrubs that make useful garden plants are actually shrublike forms of evergreen trees. These may have been selected because they are slow-growing or because they have a bushy or weeping shape. Some dwarf conifers are so small and slow-growing that they serve more the purpose of novelty plants than they do the purpose of shrubs.

Conifers are important evergreen shrubs in the North, where most broad-leaved evergreens are not hardy. They provide very important greenery during the winter months when many plants are leafless and the rest of the landscape is colorless. Conifers are also valuable and widely used plants in warmer areas of the United States where they share the landscape with broad-leaved evergreens.

Broad-leaved evergreens: The foliage of most broad-leaved evergreens is composed of flat, expanded leaves similar to those of deciduous plants. Broad-leaved evergreens are flowering plants and many kinds put out showy blossoms and fruit. Their year-round greenery is, however, of primary importance in the landscape.

Though their name does not suggest it, broad-leaved evergreens offer a variety of textures for the landscape. They can be softly textured with small leaves and arching branches as is glossy abelia, or they can be bold textured with coarse, waxy leaves as are many of the hollies. In most cases, broad-leaved evergreens have a different effect in the landscape than narrow-leaved evergreens. Leaf size and branch structure will influence the way plants fit visually in small-scale landscapes. Shrubs with a bold, busy appearance should be used with restraint in confined areas.

LANDSCAPE USES

Admired for the serenity of their low-keyed greenery, these important ornamental plants are also important problem-solvers. The following are examples of how you can best use evergreen shrubs on your property.

Accent: An accent shrub is one that because of its distinctive foliage and flowers can act as a focal point in the garden. It draws attention to itself without overwhelming the plants around it.

Background: Planted behind lower deciduous shrubs or a flower garden, evergreen shrubs set off the other plants, making an excellent green background for bright flowers or fall foliage and even for bare branches. Fine-textured evergreens make the best backgrounds.

Barrier: Evergreen shrubs with thorns, sharp needles, or very dense growth are often used to keep people and animals from going where you don't want them to.

Color: Evergreens can be many shades of green: dark green, blue-green, yellow-green, gray-green, and bright green. Some evergreens have brightly variegated foliage and others produce colorful flowers and fruits.

Definition: Evergreen shrubs can be used to emphasize the shape or size of an area. A low hedge surrounding a patio or lining a walkway accentuates its position in the landscape. Shrubs planted on either side of a door or pathway provide framing that directs the eye.

Entryways: Plants used around an entrance of a home serve as part of its welcome mat, directing visitors to the door. Many evergreen shrubs are attractive year-round—just what you want to frame your front door.

Espalier: Espalier is the art of pruning and training plants into a pattern of lines in a flat plane. Often espaliers are made against a wall or on an open trellis.

Fine-textured evergreen shrubs make excellent hedges or living fences that serve as barriers, define areas of activity, and ensure privacy. Many species can be sheared or pruned for a formal effect. The natural growth habit of many other plants will produce an informal hedge, requiring almost no pruning.

Evergreen shrubs are the backbone of home landscaping. They are used to blend buildings into the garden setting, soften architectural lines, conceal unattractive views, provide privacy, and give your home a welcoming appearance.

Foundation planting: Evergreen shrubs are invaluable for landscaping the front of a home. They conceal the foundation of the building throughout the year, blending the house into the landscape by softening harsh lines and corners.

Ground covers: Some evergreen shrubs are low, ground-hugging plants that are perfect for dressing up the ground without blocking a view or creating a visual barrier. Cloaking the ground with greenery, these plants make a low-maintenance alternative to a lawn.

Hedge: Fine-textured evergreen shrubs make the most handsome hedges. They can be pruned into a neat shape for a *formal* hedge or allowed to assume their natural shape for an *informal* hedge. Use a hedge as a low barrier, to act as a living fence, or to mark the boundary of your property.

Screen: Tall evergreen shrubs planted in formal or informal

Yews *(Taxus sp.)* are slow-growing and withstand pruning and shearing, making useful hedges, screens, or accent plants.

A border of Burford holly *(Ilex cornuta 'Burfordii')* conceals a stark fence.

Mugo pines *(Pinus mugo)* grow slowly and have dense foliage. One of the few pines that can be pruned as a topiary.

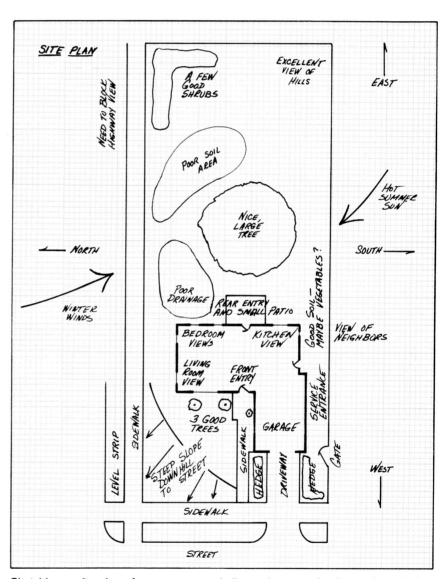

Sketching a site plan of your property, similar to the example shown above, helps you identify the landscape needs of your property. Once you note which views need to be blocked or preserved, where shade is needed, areas of poor soil or bad drainage, and paths of movement, you can begin to choose plants that meet your specific landscape requirements.

The landscaping around your home's front entrance deserves special attention. Create an attractive setting by selecting a combination of plants that will provide year-round beauty. Here, evergreen shrubs are used for hedging and in containers on the porch. They provide a permanent green background for the seasonal color of flowering trees, vines, and deciduous plants.

hedges or in shrub borders can screen unsightly views as well as provide you with privacy from your neighbors' yards.

Shrub border: People frequently beautify their landscapes by planting shrubbery around the boundary of their yards. Such a shrub border looks best if different heights and textures of plants are mixed together in curved beds rather than in straight-edged ones. Use evergreen shrubs in borders to provide privacy, as a background for deciduous plants, and for year-round greenery.

Soften architectural lines: Evergreen shrubs with horizontal branching patterns planted near the corners of a house blend it into the landscape.

Specimen plant: A free-standing plant that is so dramatic or beautiful that it doesn't need other plants to set it off is called a specimen plant. Many evergreens have dramatic character and make excellent specimens.

Stopgap-filler: A fast-growing plant used to fill a space in the garden created by an unexpected plant loss.

Topiary: Topiary is the art of pruning plants into fanciful animal or geometric shapes. Some fine-textured evergreen shrubs lend themselves to this treatment.

Transition: A planting of a group of low shrubs is often a useful way to separate different areas of a yard, creating a visual and physical transition that divides the property into separate areas.

SITE PLAN

A site plan is a sketch or diagram, drawn to scale, of your house and yard. It shows the locations of doors, windows, and rooms, as well as trees, shrubs, garden beds, and outdoor areas such as patios and walks. Other physical characteristics of your property that might affect your gardening efforts should also be noted—good and bad views from indoors and out, directions of

prevailing winds, slopes, sun patterns, and high and low spots.

Done properly, a site plan takes a good deal of time and observation. You should watch how the sun and wind patterns change with the seasons. These observations are important since some areas of your property may be in full sun in winter but be shaded in summer. Noting the growing conditions of different areas of your yard will help you choose the trees and shrubs that will serve you best.

You can make an accurate site plan using graph paper and a copy of your survey. Record landscape features not noted on the survey, such as trees and garden plots, by carefully measuring their distances from the house. Mark trees and shrubs with circles indicating their branch spread at maturity. When you have a good diagram of your property, you can place tracing paper over it and experiment with possible planting and landscaping ideas before you ever touch a shovel to the ground.

The bold textures of red brick and Japanese privets *(Ligustrum japonicum)* are attention-getting.

Rosemary *(Rosmarinus officinalis)* has fine-textured aromatic foliage and bears tiny light-blue flowers in spring.

Mugo pines *(Pinus mugo)* are dense and compact, making a low-maintenance hedge.

CHOOSING THE RIGHT EVERGREEN

After you have made a plot plan or observed your property carefully, you will notice locations where evergreen shrubs would beautify your yard and garden, or solve particular problems. The next step is deciding which shrub will do the best job in the locations where you need evergreens.

Besides trying to match the cultural needs of a particular evergreen to what the site has to offer, you should consider the visual impact the shrub will have on the location. The look of a shrub is determined by such things as its texture, color, and habit (shape). You will also want to choose a fast-growing shrub if you want quick results and a low-maintenance shrub if you haven't much time for gardening.

Texture: Conifers generally have a fine texture and broad-leaved evergreens generally have a bold texture. Particular plants though, depending upon needle or leaf size and shape, will make a slightly different impact.

A plant's texture affects the appearance of your garden. Fine-textured plants seem smaller and farther away, thus making small areas seem larger and large areas look even bigger. Bold-textured plants appear to be larger and closer than they really are. They can make distant areas seem nearer and open spaces more cozy, but if used incorrectly bold-textured plants create a crowded feeling.

Color: Evergreens offer many shades of green and these should be considered when making your choice. Try to contrast blue-greens with bright greens, for example, so the shrubs stand apart from their background and each other. Also remember that many broad-leaved evergreens produce colorful flowers for several weeks of the year—the color of the blossoms should complement your house and garden.

Habit: Some shrubs are tall and columnar, making a formal accent. Others are more spreading with horizontal branches. If possible, take a look at a mature specimen before you plant a particular shrub. Be sure its shape suits your garden.

Growth rate: Many home-owners are impatient for their plants to mature and fill in the garden, but fast-growing shrubs may soon become lanky.

Maintenance: Some shrubs require more pruning, watering, and spraying than others. Choose plants that will suit your life-style.

THE OUTDOOR ROOM

Visualizing your backyard or entryway as an outdoor room is often helpful in creating a comfortable outdoor living area. Think in three dimensions and use the same requirements you would for an indoor room. A patio, porch, deck, or lawn can be your floor. Hedges, shrubs, or fences serve as walls to provide enclosure, privacy, and a sense of security. A large tree or arbor blocks strong sunlight and is the roof. Specimen and accent plants fill blank corners. Paths allow easy access from one area to another. Barbecues and sink areas are included for the outdoor cook and there is a play area for the children. This approach may not be applicable in every yard but recreating what you like inside on the outside can make an outdoor area as livable as any indoor room.

SELECTION AID

The lists that follow will help you select appropriate shrubs for your yard. Use these lists as an introduction to the descriptions of top-rated evergreen shrubs in the encyclopedia section. Do not decide on any shrub until you have read its complete description. If a plant is listed without a specific species, such as *Cotoneaster sp.*, there are several species to choose from; referring to the individual plant entries will help you make a choice.

Combinations of needled evergreens and broad-leaved evergreens create interesting contrasts of texture, form, and color. Here evergreen shrubs frame a pleasant view and form a hedge that conceals the vegetable garden and outlines the patio. They also serve as accent, transition, and background plants to highlight seasonal color.

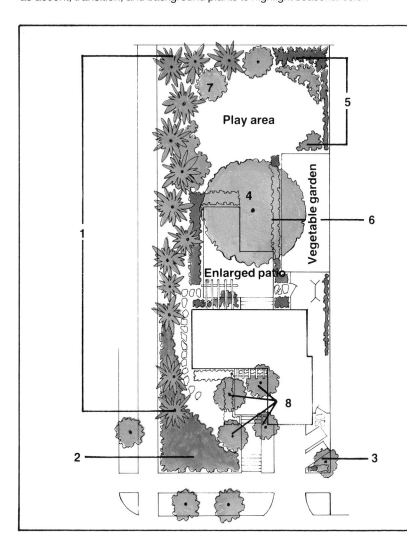

Final Landscape Plan

This example of a complete landscape plan is one way the problems identified by the site plan on page 10 might be solved.

1. Dense planting of evergreen trees blocks the unwanted view, buffers highway noise, and provides privacy.

2. Evergreen shrubs are used as a ground cover to prevent erosion on steep slope.

3. Evergreen shrubs provide hedging and screening for parking area definition.

4. A large deciduous flowering tree shades patio and house, creating a comfortable outdoor living area.

5. Low planting of evergreen shrubs frames attractive view.

6. Hedge of evergreen shrubs hides vegetable garden.

7. Evergreen shrubs and trees form a contrasting background for flowering accent tree.

8. Evergreen hedges and shrubbery provide permanent greenery; enhance seasonal color of flowering plants.

Yaupon *(Ilex vomitoria)*   Blue rug juniper *(Juniperus sp.)*   Variegated euonymus *(Euonymus sp.)*

Evergreen Shrubs Landscape Use Lists

Hedges

These shrubs respond well to frequent shearing. Use them where a full-foliaged, formal or informal hedge is desired.

		Zones
Abelia x grandiflora		
	Glossy Abelia	6-10
Berberis sp.	Barberry	5-8
Buxus sp.	Boxwood	5-10
Coprosma repens	Mirror Plant	9-10
Cotoneaster buxifolius		
	Dwarf Silver-Leaf Cotoneaster	7-10
Elaeagnus pungens	Silverberry	7-10
Euonymus sp.	Euonymus	4-9
Ilex sp.	Holly	5-10
Ligustrum sp.	Privet	7-10
Murraya paniculata		
	Orange Jessamine	9
Myrtus communis	True Myrtle	9-10
Photinia x fraseri		
	Red-Tip Photinia	7-10
Pittosporum tobira	Tobira	8-10
Prunus sp.	Flowering Fruit	7-10
Pyracantha sp.	Firethorn	5-10
Taxus sp.	Yew	5-9
Thuja sp.	Arborvitae	3-9
Viburnum tinus	Laurustinus	7-10
Xylosma congestum		
	Shiny Xylosma	8-10

Ground Covers

These evergreen shrubs are top-rated for use as ground covers. Some have more than one variety or species that can be used as a ground cover. See complete plant descriptions for information on prostrate forms.

		Zones
Abelia x grandiflora		
	Glossy Abelia	6-10
Baccharis pilularis		
	Coyote Brush	8-10
Carissa grandiflora	Natal Plum	10
Ceanothus sp.	Wild Lilac	8-10
Cotoneaster sp.	Cotoneaster	5-10
Euonymus fortunei		
	Wintercreeper	4-8
Hebe sp.	Hebe	9-10
Juniperus sp.	Juniper	3-10
Leucothoe fontanesiana		
	Drooping Leucothoe	5-8
Nandina domestica		
	Heavenly Bamboo	6-10
Pyracantha sp.	Firethorn	5-10
Raphiolepis indica		
	Indian Hawthorn	8-10
Rosmarinus officinalis		
	Rosemary	7-10
Sarcococca hookerana humilis		
	Sweet Box	7-10
Taxus baccata	English Yew	6-9

Entryways

Entryways are special landscape situations that call for plants that look good all the time. Here are some of the best evergreen shrubs to help form your landscaped welcome mat.

		Zones
Abelia x grandiflora		
	Glossy Abelia	6-10
Camellia sp.	Camellia	7-10
Cleyera japonica		
	Japanese Cleyera	8-10
Euonymus sp.	Euonymus	4-9
Gardenia jasminoides	Gardenia	8-10
Grevillea 'Noell'		
	Noell Grevillea	8-10
Ilex sp.	Holly	5-10
Nandina domestica		
	Heavenly Bamboo	6-10
Picea abies	Norway Spruce	2-8
Pieris sp.	Pieris	5-9
Pinus mugo	Mugo Pine	2-8
Platycladus orientalis		
	Oriental Arborvitae	6-10
Raphiolepis indica		
	Indian Hawthorn	8-10
Rhododendron hybrids	Azalea	6-10
Sarcococca hookerana humilis		
	Sweet Box	7-10
Skimmia japonica		
	Japanese Skimmia	6-8
Taxus sp.	Yew	5-9
Thuja occidentalis		
	American Arborvitae	3-9
Tsuga canadensis 'Pendula'		
	Sargent Weeping Hemlock	5-9

Indian hawthorn *(Raphiolepis indica)*

Japanese skimmia *(Skimmia japonica)*

Red-tip photinia *(Photinia x fraseri)*

Attractive Flowers

These shrubs deserve a visible spot in the landscape where their blossoms can be appreciated. Those marked with an * have fragrant flowers.

		Zones
Camellia sp.	Camellia	7-10
*Carissa grandiflora**	Natal Plum	10
*Ceanothus sp.**	Wild Lilac	8-10
*Cistus x purpureus**		
	Orchid-Spot Rock Rose	8-10
Cotoneaster sp.	Cotoneaster	5-10
*Gardenia jasminoides**		
	Gardenia	8-10
*Grevillea 'Noell'**		
	Noell Grevillea	8-10
Hibiscus rosa-sinensis		
	Chinese Hibiscus	9-10
*Leucothoe sp.**	Leucothoe	5-9
*Ligustrum japonicum**		
	Japanese Privet	7-10
Mahonia sp.	Mahonia	5-10
*Murraya paniculata**		
	Orange Jessamine	9
*Myrtus communis**	True Myrtle	9-10
Nerium oleander	Oleander	8-10
Photinia x fraseri		
	Red-Tip Photinia	7-10
Pieris sp.	Pieris	5-9
*Pittosporum tobira**	Tobira	8-10
*Prunus sp.**	Flowering Fruit	7-10
Pyracantha sp.	Firethorn	5-10
Raphiolepis indica		
	Indian Hawthorn	8-10
Rhododendron hybrids		
	Azalea, Rhododendron	4-10
Rosmarinus officinalis		
	Rosemary	7-10
*Sarcococca hookerana humilis**		
	Sweet Box	7-10
Skimmia japonica		
	Japanese Skimmia	6-8
*Viburnum sp.**	Viburnum	7-10

Fragrant Flowers

The following evergreen shrubs have inconspicuous but fragrant flowers.

		Zones
Cleyera japonica		
	Japanese Cleyera	8-10
Elaeagnus pungens		
	Silverberry	7-10
Osmanthus heterophyllus		
	Holly Olive	7-10

Colorful Fruit

Brightly colored fruit can be a striking and long-lasting landscape attraction.

		Zones
Carissa grandiflora	Natal Plum	10
Cotoneaster sp.	Cotoneaster	5-10
Euonymus sp.	Euonymus	4-9
Ilex sp.	Holly	5-10
Mahonia sp.	Mahonia	5-10
Murraya paniculata		
	Orange Jessamine	9
Nandina domestica		
	Heavenly Bamboo	6-10
Photinia x fraseri		
	Red-Tip Photinia	7-10
Pittosporum tobira	Tobira	8-10
Pyracantha sp.	Firethorn	5-10
Sarcococca hookerana humilis		
	Sweet Box	7-10
Skimmia japonica		
	Japanese Skimmia	6-8
Taxus sp.	Yew	5-9
Viburnum sp.	Viburnum	7-10

Colorful Foliage

These evergreen shrubs have colorful foliage or are available in variegated forms.

		Zones
Abelia x grandiflora		
	Glossy Abelia	6-10
Callistemon citrinus		
	Lemon Bottlebrush	8-10
Coprosma repens	Mirror Plant	9-10
Euonymus fortunei		
	Wintercreeper	4-8
Ilex aquifolium	English Holly	6-9
Leucothoe fontanesiana		
	Drooping Leucothoe	5-8
Mahonia sp.	Mahonia	5-10
Myrtus communis	True Myrtle	9-10
Nandina domestica		
	Heavenly Bamboo	6-10
Photinia x fraseri		
	Red-Tip Photinia	7-10
Pieris japonica	Andromeda	5-9
Pittosporum tobira	Tobira	8-10
Platycladus orientalis		
	Oriental Arborvitae	6-10
Raphiolepis indica		
	Indian Hawthorn	8-10
Thuja occidentalis		
	American Arborvitae	3-9
Xylosma congestum		
	Shiny Xylosma	8-10

Chinese holly *(Ilex cornuta)*

Shiny xylosma *(Xylosma congestum)*

Firethorn *(Pyracantha sp.)*

Barrier Plantings

These shrubs can be used to keep people and animals from going where you don't want them. All are dense. Many have thorns.

		Zones
Berberis sp.	Barberry	5-8
Carissa grandiflora	Natal Plum	10
Elaeagnus pungens	Silverberry	7-10
Ilex sp.	Holly	5-10
Juniperus sp.	Juniper	3-10
Mahonia sp.	Mahonia	5-10
Pyracantha sp.	Firethorn	5-10

Fast-Growing

		Zones
Baccharis pilularis		
	Coyote Brush	8-10
Berberis sp.	Barberry	5-8
Ceanothus sp.	Wild Lilac	8-10
Cistus x purpureus		
	Orchid-Spot Rock Rose	8-10
Coprosma repens	Mirror Plant	9-10
Cotoneaster dammeri		
	Bearberry Cotoneaster	5-10
Dodonaea viscosa	Hopbush	8-10
Elaeagnus pungens	Silverberry	7-10
Juniperus sp.	Juniper	3-10
Ligustrum japonicum		
	Japanese Privet	7-10
Myoporum laetum 'Carsonii'		
	Myoporum	8-10
Nerium oleander	Oleander	8-10
Prunus laurocerasus		
	English Laurel	7-10
Pyracantha coccinea		
	Scarlet Firethorn	5-9

Grow in Shade

Some shrubs grow best in shade. Others tolerate shade but grow best in full sun. Check a plant's full description to learn its best adaptation.

		Zones
Buxus sp.	Boxwood	5-10
Camellia sp.	Camellia	7-10
Carissa grandiflora	Natal Plum	10
Chamaecyparis sp.		
	False Cypress	5-9
Cleyera japonica		
	Japanese Cleyera	8-10
Cocculus laurifolius		
	Laurel-Leaf Cocculus	8-10
Coprosma repens	Mirror Plant	9-10
Euonymus sp.	Euonymus	4-9
Gardenia jasminoides	Gardenia	8-10
Ilex sp.	Holly	5-10
Leucothoe sp.	Leucothoe	5-9
Ligustrum japonicum		
	Japanese Privet	7-10
Mahonia sp.	Mahonia	5-10
Murraya paniculata		
	Orange Jessamine	9
Myrtus communis	True Myrtle	9-10
Nandina domestica		
	Heavenly Bamboo	6-10
Osmanthus heterophyllus		
	Holly Olive	7-10
Pieris sp.	Pieris	5-9
Pittosporum tobira	Tobira	8-10
Rhododendron hybrids		
	Azalea, Rhododendron	4-10
Sarcococca hookerana humilis		
	Sweet Box	7-10
Skimmia japonica		
	Japanese Skimmia	6-8
Taxus sp.	Yew	5-9
Viburnum sp.	Viburnum	7-10
Xylosma congestum		
	Shiny Xylosma	8-10

Espalier

These evergreen shrubs lend themselves to espalier. Espaliers are plants trained in a flat plane by tying branches to a wall or trellis, usually in geometric patterns.

		Zones
Camellia sp.	Camellia	7-10
Carissa grandiflora	Natal Plum	10
Cocculus laurifolius		
	Laurel-Leaf Cocculus	8-10
Coprosma repens	Mirror Plant	9-10
Elaeagnus pungens	Silverberry	7-10
Euonymus fortunei		
	Wintercreeper	4-8
Gardenia jasminoides		
	Gardenia	8-10
Hibiscus rosa-sinensis		
	Chinese Hibiscus	9-10
Ilex x altaclarensis 'Wilsonii'		
	Wilson Holly	6-10
Ilex cornuta 'Burfordii'		
	Burford Holly	6-10
Photinia x fraseri		
	Red-Tip Photinia	7-10
Pyracantha sp.	Firethorn	5-10
Sarcococca hookerana humilis		
	Sweet Box	7-10
Xylosma congestum		
	Shiny Xylosma	8-10

Cotoneaster *(Cotoneaster sp.)* and juniper *(Juniperus sp.)*

Cotoneaster *(Cotoneaster sp.)*

Tobira *(Pittosporum tobira)*

Cold-Hardy

Here are some of the hardiest evergreen shrubs for cold climates.

		Zones
Berberis sp.	Barberry	5-8
Chamaecyparis sp.		
	False Cypress	5-9
Cotoneaster dammeri		
	Bearberry Cotoneaster	5-10
Euonymus fortunei		
	Wintercreeper	4-8
Juniperus sp.	Juniper	3-10
Leucothoe fontanesiana		
	Drooping Leucothoe	5-8
Mahonia sp.	Mahonia	5-10
Picea abies	Norway Spruce	2-8
Pieris sp.	Andromeda	5-9
Pinus mugo	Mugo Pine	2-8
Rhododendron hybrids		
	Rhododendron	4-10
Taxus sp.	Yew	5-9
Thuja occidentalis		
	American Arborvitae	3-9

Windbreaks

These are sturdy evergreen shrubs that can stand up to strong winds.

		Zones
Dodonaea viscosa	Hopbush	8-10
Elaeagnus pungens	Silverberry	7-10
Juniperus sp.	Juniper	3-10
Ligustrum japonicum		
	Japanese Privet	7-10
Myoporum laetum 'Carsonii'		
	Myoporum	8-10
Nerium oleander	Oleander	8-10
Pittosporum tobira	Tobira	8-10
Prunus sp.	Flowering Fruit	7-10
Pyracantha sp.	Firethorn	5-10
Taxus sp.	Yew	5-9
Thuja occidentalis		
	American Arborvitae	3-9

Tolerate Seashore Conditions

These shrubs can withstand the winds and moist, salty air of coastal areas. Those marked with an * will grow in the harsh climatic conditions of the Pacific Coast.

		Zones
*Baccharis pilularis**		
	Coyote Brush	8-10
Berberis julianae		
	Wintergreen Barberry	6-8
*Carissa grandiflora**	Natal Plum	10
*Ceanothus sp.**	Wild Lilac	8-10
*Cistus x purpureus**		
	Orchid-Spot Rock Rose	8-10
*Coprosma repens**	Mirror Plant	9-10
Cotoneaster dammeri		
	Bearberry Cotoneaster	5-10
*Dodonaea viscosa**	Hopbush	8-10
*Elaeagnus pungens**		
	Silverberry	7-10
*Euonymus japonica**		
	Evergreen Euonymus	7-9
Ilex crenata	Japanese Holly	5-10
*Juniperus sp.**	Juniper	3-10
Leucothoe sp.	Leucothoe	5-9
Myoporum laetum 'Carsonii' *		
	Myoporum	8-10
*Pinus mugo**	Mugo Pine	2-8
Pyracantha coccinea		
	Scarlet Firethorn	5-9
*Raphiolepis indica**		
	Indian Hawthorn	8-10
*Rosmarinus officinalis**		
	Rosemary	7-10
Taxus sp.	Yew	5-9

Heat-Resistant, Drought-Tolerant

These shrubs are star performers in hot climates. Use them in the desert as well as in hot southern or western exposures around any home. Those marked with an * are drought-tolerant. However, occasional watering will keep them looking their best.

		Zones
*Baccharis pilularis**		
	Coyote Brush	8-10
*Callistemon sp.**	Bottlebrush	8-10
*Ceanothus sp.**	Wild Lilac	8-10
*Cistus x purpureus**		
	Orchid-Spot Rock Rose	8-10
*Coprosma repens**	Mirror Plant	9-10
Cotoneaster sp.	Cotoneaster	5-10
*Dodonaea viscosa**	Hopbush	8-10
*Elaeagnus pungens**		
	Silverberry	7-10
Hibiscus rosa-sinensis		
	Chinese Hibiscus	9-10
*Juniperus sp.**	Juniper	3-10
*Ligustrum japonicum**		
	Japanese Privet	7-10
*Nerium oleander**	Oleander	8-10
Photinia x fraseri		
	Red-Tip Photinia	7-10
*Pittosporum tobira**	Tobira	8-10
*Prunus caroliniana**		
	Carolina Cherry Laurel	7-10
*Pyracantha sp.**	Firethorn	5-10
*Rosmarinus officinalis**		
	Rosemary	7-10
*Taxus sp.**	Yew	5-9
*Xylosma congestum**		
	Shiny Xylosma	8-10

Ceanothus
California Lilac, Wild Lilac

Zones: 8-10. To 5-20 feet. Flowering.

The majority of the evergreen species are natives of California where many improved varieties have been developed. Blue flowers, the rarest color for hardy shrubs, are the major attraction of wild lilac. They are sun-loving plants to use as ground and bank covers, for screening, or as specimens without irrigation.

Plant sizes vary from prostrate spreaders to rounded shrubs to small broad trees. Leaves are bright green. Flowers range from white to deep purple-blue and open from March to May depending on the variety. Once ceanothus is established, avoid summer watering, which will encourage root-rot diseases.

Chamaecyparis
False Cypress

There are 6 species of evergreen trees in this genus, 3 from North America and 3 from Japan. Numerous dwarf cultivars that make useful shrubs are available. Grow in full sunshine as they tend to become leggy in heavy shade. A site with adequate moisture and good drainage is required for best growth. Fertilization can destroy some dwarfness. A neutral to slightly acid soil and a humid atmosphere are preferred. Plant in locations protected from strong winds.

Chamaecyparis obtusa
Hinoki False Cypress
Zones: 5-9. To 50-75 feet.

This conifer is a handsome plant with fan-shaped branches of dark green scalelike foliage. Many dwarf or very slow-growing forms that are suitable for rock gardens, foundation plantings, border plantings, or specimen plants for small properties are available. Many are grown as container plants or bonsai.

The cultivar 'Nana' is one of the shortest, slowest-growing forms and

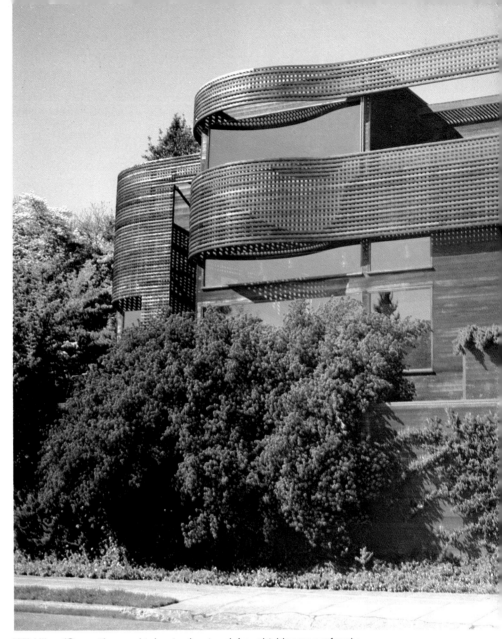

Wild lilac *(Ceanothus sp.)* tolerates heat and drought; blooms profusely.

False cypress *(Chamaecyparis sp.)*

There are many dwarf varieties of false cypress (*Chamaecyparis sp.*) with uniquely different foliage and form.

Orchid-spot rock rose (*Cistus x purpureus*) is a fire-resistant plant. It tolerates drought and coastal conditions.

Laurel-leaf cocculus (*Cocculus laurifolius*)

may reach 2 to 3 feet in 60 years. 'Nana Gracilis', often sold as 'Nana', will reach 9 feet in 60 years. Both cultivars are compact and bushy when young. 'Nana Gracilis' becomes pyramidal as it matures. 'Kosteri' will grow to 4 feet high; its foliage sprays are twisted at the branch tips, presenting a cupped appearance; pruning is required to develop a single-stemmed plant. 'Nana Lutea' is a dwarf whose foliage is yellow when grown in sun.

Chamaecyparis pisifera
Sawara False Cypress
Zones: 5-9. To 1-20 feet.

Some of the numerous horticultural varieties of false cypress available are so different it is difficult to believe they all originated from the same species. Some plants have threadlike, long slender twigs with few branchings, others have feathery foliage, some have long slender needles that do not clasp the stem, and some forms are dwarf. Many of these dwarfs are slow-growing when young but accelerate growth after a few years and end up being sizeable plants.

The cultivar 'Filifera' has weeping, threadlike bluish-green foliage. A similar, golden-foliaged cultivar, 'Filifera Aurea', is often planted as a dwarf but will eventually reach 18 feet or more in height. 'Squarrosa Minima' is also sold as 'Pygmaea'. Plants vary but are generally very dwarf, from 6 to 18 inches high.

Cistus x purpureus
Orchid-Spot Rock Rose
Zones: 8-10. To 3-4 feet.
Flowering.

Orchid-spot rock rose is a fast-growing sun- and drought-tolerant hybrid between *C. lananiferus* and *C. villosus*. Use as a cover for dry banks, as a low divider, or for erosion control. A fire-resistant plant, it is recommended for planting in areas of fire hazard. It also withstands cold ocean winds and salt sprays.

Orchid-spot rock rose is a compact shrub growing to 4 feet tall and 4 feet wide. Leaves are rich green above and hairy gray beneath. Resembling a small single rose, the 3-inch flowers are lavender with maroon blotches at petal bases and numerous yellow stamens. Flowering is continuous during June and July. Needs sun and well-drained soil.

Cleyera japonica (Eurya ochnacea)
Japanese Cleyera
Zones: 8-10. To 15-18 feet.
Flowering.

The leaves of this handsome foliage shrub are brownish red when new, turn to dark glossy green in summer, and change to reddish in winter. Small creamy-white flowers are followed by dark red berries.

Cocculus laurifolius
Laurel-Leaf Cocculus, Laurel-Leaf Snailseed
Zones: 8-10. To 10-25 feet.

This foliage plant from the Himalayas has bright glossy green leaves. It can take several different forms. Without pruning, it becomes an arching multistemmed shrub, spreading as wide as tall, useful for a screen or background plant. With pruning, it can be a low shrub or be trained as an espalier.

An adaptable plant, it will grow in sun or shade. Growth is more open with shading. It tolerates many soil types but must have a continuous supply of moisture to grow well.

Convolvulus cneorum
Bush Morning-Glory
Zones: 7-10. To 2-4 feet.
Flowering.

Bush morning-glory is a fast-growing shrub for dry areas. It has smooth gray leaves and yellow-throated, trumpet-shaped white or pink flowers all summer. Grow in full sun. Can be grown in groups, in borders, or on banks.

Coprosma repens (C. baueri)
Mirror Plant, Taupata

Zones: 9-10. To 10-25 feet.

This is a lovely foliage plant whose dark to light green leaves have extremely glossy surfaces. It is native to the warm coastal regions of New Zealand, where plant height varies from prostrate in exposed areas to a small tree when sheltered. Use as a hedge, screen, or tall ground cover. Plant in full sun or partial shade and water regularly. Drought-tolerant once established. A good coastal plant.

Cotoneaster
Cotoneaster

Cotoneasters are popular and adaptable shrubs, ranging in size from prostrate ground covers to tall arching shrubs. There are both evergreen and deciduous species. They are dense, twiggy plants covered with small oval leaves. Dainty white to pinkish flowers line the branches in spring and are attractive but not showy. Long-lasting red berries in fall and winter are the outstanding feature. Berry production will be heavier in dry soil than in a fertile, well-watered garden. Growth is best in full sun although some will grow in partial shade. Use for ground covers and erosion control and as foreground plants in shrub borders or foundation plantings.

Fireblight, caused by a bacteria, can be a problem with cotoneaster.

Cotoneaster buxifolius
Dwarf Silver-Leaf Cotoneaster
Zones: 7-10. To 1-2 feet.
Flowering.

This plant's name is C. buxifolius but it is widely sold as C. glaucophyllus, which means "white leaves". It is native to India, where it has white leaves, and to western China, where it has dull green leaves. Plants derived from both sources can be found in nurseries. Leaves of the white-foliaged form are covered with white hairs on both

Bearberry cotoneaster *(Cotoneaster dammeri)* makes a handsome ground cover, good cascading plant for walls. Flowers shown below.

Silverberry (Elaeagnus pungens), in mid-ground, bears fragrant blooms in fall followed by showy berries. Silver-dotted leaves, shown below, reflect sunlight.

surfaces. The leaves of the dull green-foliaged type have tan fuzz on the bottom.

Clusters of 1 to 3 flowers form bright red berries in fall. Most plants become dense mounds but prostrate forms are also grown. White-leaved forms make good accent plants.

Cotoneaster congestus
Pyrenees Cotoneaster
Zones: 6-10. To 3 feet.
Flowering.

A dense, rounded mound with branches curving downward, this cotoneaster generally grows about 8 inches a year. Round leaves, 1/3 inch long, are a dull dark green above and whitish beneath. Pinkish-white 1/4-inch flowers line the branches and are followed by 1/4-inch bright red berries.

Cotoneaster dammeri
Bearberry Cotoneaster
Zones: 5-10. To 3-15 inches.
Flowering.

This low, spreading shrub is top-rated as a ground cover or for cascading over rocks and walls where it softens their appearance. Long trailing branches root at the nodes as they quickly spread. A single plant can easily grow 10 feet wide. If the plants are top-dressed with compost or bark to encourage stem rooting, they will spread even wider. It grows and fruits best in full sun but does well in partial shade.

Dark, glossy green oval leaves measure up to 1 inch long. The white flowers appear in May or June and are the showiest of the cotoneasters. Berries, up to 1/2 inch across, ripen to a glossy red in October and November.

Many selections with improved characteristics are available. 'Coral Beauty' produces abundant coral-colored berries. 'Lowfast' is fast spreading and remains low, 4 to 8 inches tall. 'Mooncreeper' is also low and spreading. 'Royal Beauty' hugs the ground and bears deep red berries. 'Skogholmen' is very fast spreading and more open. It reaches 15 inches tall.

Cotoneaster lacteus (C. parneyi)
Red Clusterberry Cotoneaster
Zones: 7-10. To 6-10 feet.
Flowering.

This arching, upright plant becomes twice as wide as tall. Leaves are 1-1/2 to 3 inches long, dull green, and markedly veined above, with white hairs beneath. Flowers form in clusters 2 to 3 inches wide along the stems. Clusters of 1/4-inch dark red berries remain colorful throughout winter.

This species will grow in dry areas. It is useful for screen plantings, espaliering, or as a clipped hedge. Cut berry sprays make pretty arrangements.

Dodonaea viscosa
Hopbush, Hopseed Bush
Zones: 8-10. To 10-15 feet.
Flowering.

This large fast-growing, multi-stemmed shrub has flaking bark and spreads almost as wide as tall. Leaves are willowlike. The flowers are not showy but female plants have attractive creamy or pinkish winged fruit in late summer. It is planted for hedges, informal screens, espaliers, or as a small tree. *D. viscosa* 'Purpurea', purple hopseed bush, is a purple-leaved form that is best in full sun and cool climates.

Elaeagnus pungens
Silverberry
Zones: 7-10. To 6-15 feet.
Flowering.

The most striking feature of silverberry is its silver-dotted leaves that reflect sunlight, creating a flashy effect in the landscape. It is a very fast-growing and adaptable shrub that can be clipped for a hedge or espalier and makes an effective barrier or screen. In a container silverberry withstands reflected heat and wind.

Oval leaves, 2 to 4 inches long, are grayish green above and silver below with silvery-brown dots on both surfaces. Fragrant flowers in fall are not showy but the red berries that follow, which are covered with silver scales, are eye-catching. Cultivars with variegated leaves provide even greater color interest.

'Maculata' has a yellow blotch in the center of the leaf. 'Tricolor' has yellow and pinkish-white leaf margins. 'Variegata' has yellowish-white margins.

Silverberries grow in soil that can be either slightly acid or alkaline. They tolerate both seashore and desert conditions. Established plants will tolerate drought.

Escallonia x exoniensis
Escallonia
Zones: 7-10. To 5-10 feet.
Flowering.

Pinkish blossoms borne nearly throughout the year and clean, shiny green foliage make this an attractive shrub. It can be sheared as a hedge, used as a screen, or espaliered. Tolerates wind and coastal conditions. Grows best in partial shade in hot climates, full sun in cool areas. Water regularly for best appearance.

Euonymus
Euonymus
This genus is popular for its variety of forms and handsome glossy foliage. Serviceable and easily grown, the shrubs reach mature size in 8 to 10 years. Though their flowers are insignificant, some varieties have such brightly variegated leaves that few plants can match them for year-round garden color. Mature plants may have bright orange fruit in fall and winter.

Euonymus is adaptable to a broad range of garden conditions, growing well in all but the wettest soils. They are heat-tolerant in sun or shade and are a fine choice for seashore and city gardens.

Mildew may be a problem in moist, shaded locations. Sucking insect pests, especially scale, may also be troublesome.

Variegated evergreen euonymus (Euonymus japonica 'Aureo-marginata') makes a colorful accent plant.

The white-rimmed leaves of emerald gaiety wintercreeper (Euonymus fortunei 'Emerald Gaiety') make a crisp color contrast to all-green shrubs.

29

Many variegated forms of evergreen euonymus *(Euonymus japonica)* are available. 'Aureo-marginata' (left); 'Silver King' (right).

Japanese aralia *(Fatsia japonica)* grows well in shade. Adds a tropical look to shrub borders or entryways.

Euonymus fortunei
Wintercreeper
Zones: 4-8. To 3-6 feet.

Wintercreeper and its varieties are low-growing, spreading, or compact shrubs or vines. Shrub forms are particularly well suited for foundation and border plantings. Some varieties bear brilliant orange fruit in fall and winter. Cold hardy and tolerant of most soils, wintercreeper needs good air circulation in moist areas to prevent mildew.

The following are some of the most popular varieties. 'Carrierei' is a handsome semiprostrate or clinging shrub. 'Colorata' forms a semiprostrate shrub, spreading to 4 feet; leaves are red-purple in fall and winter. 'Emerald Gaiety' is a dense, mounding, vinelike shrub with white-edged leaves. 'Emerald 'n Gold', a compact, mounding shrub to 3 feet, with bold yellow margins on dark, glossy leaves, makes a good accent plant. 'Emerald Surprise' is a vigorous low-growing shrub to 3 feet with large leaves colored green, gold, and creamy-white. 'Gracilis', a vinelike shrub, is hardy and dense; leaves are white-edged turning pink in winter; good in containers and on banks. 'Sarcoxie' is an upright shrub to 4 feet with dark green leaves.

Euonymus japonica
Evergreen Euonymus
Zones: 7-9. To 8-15 feet.

Esteemed for its neat, glossy, often brightly variegated foliage, evergreen euonymus is widely used in warm winter gardens as a medium-sized shrub or small tree. Its versatility and adaptability to a range of garden conditions make this a popular low-maintenance shrub. With a spread to 8 feet wide, evergreen euonymus makes an excellent clipped hedge, foundation or border plant. Tolerates seashore conditions.

The following are a few of the top-rated varieties. 'Aureo-marginata' is a colorful shrub, 8 to 10 feet tall, with green leaves edged bright gold. 'Aureo-variegata' features brightly colored leaves with yellow centers and green margins;

forms a compact upright shrub to 10 feet. 'Golden Queen' has large glossy leaves with rich yellow edges; this showy evergreen shrub grows to 8 feet. 'Grandifolia' is one of the most popular because of its large, shiny deep green leaves; grows fast, to 8 to 10 feet, and responds well to pruning. 'Microphylla' grows compactly to 2 feet with small boxwood-like leaves; makes an outstanding dwarf shrub for edging and small areas. 'Silver King' has beautiful green leaves with silvery-white margins and an upright habit to 10 feet. 'Silver Queen' has large, shiny dark green leaves with creamy-white margins.

Euonymus kiautschovica 'Manhattan'
Spreading Euonymus
Zones: 6-9. To 9 feet.

This outstanding shrub is prized for its large, glossy deep green leaves that are less leathery than those of most euonymus. It has a broadly spreading shape, to 9 feet tall. Bears bright red fruit in winter. Tolerates heat if watered regularly. May suffer winter damage in coldest regions. Can be sheared to create a handsome form or neat screen.

Fatsia japonica
Japanese Aralia
Zones: 8-10. To 5-10 feet.
Flowering.

Fatsia is a shade plant with a bold tropical appearance. Its leaves are broad 9- to 15-inch open fans with deeply cut oval lobes held flat on long stalks. In fall, rounded clusters of creamy-white flowers appear above the foliage. Plant in a shaded shrub border or beside an entryway. Makes a good houseplant.

Nearly any garden soil is suitable for growing Japanese aralia, though organic matter should be added when planting. Water freely where summers are warm, and shelter from hot sun. Growth is vigorous—mature plants are 5 to 10 feet tall but can be kept lower. Remove lopsided branches to create a uniform shape. The selection 'Moseri' is a dwarf compact variety. 'Variegata' has creamy-white leaf margins and needs more shade.

Gardenia jasminoides

Gardenia

Zones: 8-10. To 1-8 feet. Flowering.

These small to medium-sized shrubs from China are renowned for the memorable fragrance of their blossoms. The intensely aromatic white flowers are 1 to 5 inches across. Dark green, thick, shiny oval leaves are 2 to 4 inches long.

Growth habit varies from low and spreading to upright and open, depending on the variety. Some varieties make excellent hedges and screens. Others are suitable for containers or espaliers. All make stunning specimens.

Gardenias grow best in shade. In cool climates they can take full sun, but generally the warmer the climate, the more shade they need. They prefer a well-drained, acid soil with ample organic matter. Good growth and flowering require summer warmth, ample water, and frequent light applications of an acid fertilizer. Prune to remove straggly branches and old flowers.

'Mystery' has large 4- to 5-inch flowers, borne May to July, and is relatively open-branched, growing to 6 to 8 feet. 'Radicans' grows 6 to 12 inches tall and 2 to 3 feet wide. It has small leaves and 1-inch flowers in late spring. 'Veitchii' is a compact, upright 3- to 4-1/2-foot plant with many 1-1/2-inch flowers blooming from May to November.

Grevillea 'Noell'

Noell Grevillea

Zones: 8-10. To 3-4 feet. Flowering.

Until it blooms, this compact hybrid grevillea resembles a juniper. It grows 4 feet tall and 4 feet wide. The narrow 1-inch-long leaves are glossy green. Clusters of rose-red and white flowers open over a long period in spring. Tolerates drought. Avoid wet soil.

Gardenia *(Gardenia jasminoides)* varieties have many landscape uses. Some make excellent hedges, perfuming the garden with their fragrant flowers for many months.

Noell grevillea *(Grevillea* 'Noell') is drought-tolerant. Bears rose-red and white flowers for an extended period in spring.

31

Hebe (Hebe sp.) is widely used in mild climates as a hedge, specimen plant, and in borders.

Tropical hibiscus (Hibiscus rosa-sinensis) is a multipurpose landscape plant in mild climates. Flowers, below, bloom in summer.

Hebe

Hebe

These broad-leaved evergreen shrubs are frequently used in the mild areas of California and the South. They are valued for their neat foliage and their red to blue, late-blooming flowers. Closely related to *Veronica*, they are often mislabeled as such. Hebe grows best in cool climates in full sun, with a moist but well-drained soil. They are useful in windy coastal conditions. In warmer climates, plant in partial shade. Use in shrub borders, as low hedges, or as specimen plants.

Hebe elliptica
Zones: 9-10. To 5-6 feet.
Flowering.

This densely branched shrub has small 1-inch green leaves. Fragrant blue flowers are borne in 1- to 2-inch clusters in summer.

Hebe menziesii
Zones: 9-10. To 5 feet.
Flowering.

With a more spreading habit than most hebe, this species can be used as a tall ground cover. Has neat, tightly packed, lustrous green foliage and white flower clusters in summer.

In addition to the above species, the following hybrids are top-rated: 'Autumn Glory' is a tight, mounding plant with a neat, symmetrical shape to 2 feet high. 'Coed' has attractive dark green foliage densely packed on reddish stems. Grows to 3 feet high. 'Patty's Purple' has small dark green leaves on reddish stems. Reaches 3 feet high. 'Reevesii' features mixed reddish-purple and green foliage.

Hibiscus rosa-sinensis

Chinese Hibiscus, Tropical Hibiscus

Zones: 9-10. To 4-15 feet.
Flowering.

Hibiscus are beautiful plants with spectacular, vividly colored, tropical-looking flowers that appear throughout summer. In mild climates they are versatile landscape plants. In cold climates they must be planted in containers and moved to protected areas or indoors in winter. Hibiscus has many landscape uses in frost-free climates. They can be used as screen plants, container plants, espaliers, or specimen shrubs and small trees.

Growth habit varies from dense and compact to loose and open. In tropical areas, shrubs can reach 30 feet tall. Glossy, pointed oval leaves differ in size and texture with the variety. Large flowers, 4 to 8 inches wide, may be single or double with smooth or ruffled petals. Colors include white, red, yellow, and orange, with many multicolor blends.

Hibiscus require good soil drainage. If your soil does not drain well, plant in raised beds or containers. Flowering is best in full sun except in hot inland areas where afternoon shade is preferred. Protect plants from strong winds. Warm temperatures are required for flower production. Water thoroughly and frequently. Fertilize plants monthly from April through August. Feed container plants twice a month.

Pinch and remove irregular branches to develop good branch structure on young plants. Remove one third of the old wood on mature plants in early spring to encourage vigorous growth.

Ilex

Holly

Versatile, choice landscape plants, hollies are available in a variety of leaf shapes, textures, and growth habits. Though the common image of a holly is a large plant with shiny thorny leaves and red berries in the winter, there are also small hollies with spineless leaves, and hollies with yellow, orange, or black berries. Hollies can be used as single specimens in foundation and border plantings or as screens or hedges. Dwarf forms make good tall ground covers or container plants.

Most holly plants are either male or female and usually both sexes must be planted near each other for berries to set on female plants. A few exceptional varieties set berries without pollenization but most of these berries are small and don't last long. One male plant, with cooperation from bees, can ensure berries on up to 30 female plants of the same species.

Ilex x altaclarensis 'Wilsonii'
Wilson Holly
Zones: 6-10. To 6-20 feet.

Wilson holly is one of the best hollies for warm regions. Spiny leathery dark green leaves are 5 inches long and 3 inches wide. Produces large clusters of bright red berries. Usually a broad, dense shrub 6 to 8 feet tall, it can be grown as a 20-foot single-stemmed tree. It can also be used as a clipped hedge or espalier. Wilson holly withstands sun, shade, and wind in most soils and is somewhat drought-tolerant.

Ilex aquifolium
English Holly, Christmas Holly
Zones: 6-9. To 4-40 feet.

This is the traditional Christmas holly. Usually grown as a small tree, it can be kept pruned to form a shrub or hedge under 4 feet tall. English holly is highly variable in leaf shape and form, with some varieties having small narrow leaves and others long broad leaves. There are varieties with smooth leaves and some with spines on the surfaces and margins. Leaves may have margins or centers colored silver or gold, or be all yellow when grown in the sun. Berries formed on the female trees are red, orange, or yellow.

English holly needs protection from direct sun in hot, dry areas. Soil should be acid. Leaf miners can be troublesome.

There are many cultivars of English holly. 'Balkans' is the hardiest; it has an upright growth habit and dark green spineless leaves. 'Sparkler' has an upright habit and produces an abundance of bright red berries. 'Argenteo-marginata' and 'Silver Queen' have leaves edged with white. 'Aureo-marginata' has gold-edged leaves.

Chinese holly *(Ilex cornuta)* has a crisp, fresh look. It serves a variety of uses in the landscape.

Holly *(Ilex sp.)* varieties offer a wide choice of leaf sizes and shapes, and growth forms.

Dwarf Burford holly (Ilex cornuta 'Burfordii Nana') in the background and dwarf yaupon (I. vomitoria 'Nana') in the foreground make an effective low border.

Pfitzer juniper (Juniperus chinensis 'Pfitzerana') grows rapidly. Can reach 6 feet tall and spread to 15 feet.

Ilex cornuta
Chinese Holly
Zones: 6-10. To 2-10 feet.

A broad shrub or compact small tree, Chinese holly typically has glossy, stiff, nearly rectangular leaves. Spines are generally at the four corners and tip but varieties differ in spinyness and leaf shape. A long warm season is needed to ripen the large red berries. Female selections will set fruit in varying amounts without a pollinator. Protection from sun is needed in desert climates.

'Burfordii' grows to 10 to 14 feet. Its nearly spineless dark green leaves are cupped downward; produces heavy crops of brilliant red berries; makes a good espalier. 'Burfordii Nana' is much smaller than 'Burfordii' with small light green spineless leaves; bears numerous berries. 'Dazzler' is a compact, upright 8- to 12-foot holly; its glossy deep green leaves have stout spines; fruits heavily. 'Rotunda' is a dense, compact, low-growing plant that doesn't fruit; nearly rectangular light green leaves are medium-sized and spiny.

Ilex crenata
Japanese Holly
Zones: 5-10. To 2-15 feet.

A dense shrub with small, fine-textured leaves, Japanese holly looks more like a boxwood than a typical holly. It is an excellent shiny-leaved evergreen for hedges, foundation plantings, or backgrounds in cold climates. Grows well in urban areas. Leaves are 1/2 to 3/4 inch long, flat or cupped downward. Typically, the small berries are black and inconspicuous, but yellow-berried forms are known.

Basically Japanese holly is adapted to Zones 6 to 10. However, there are two top-rated varieties that will grow into Zone 5. They are: 'Green Luster', a dense and compact plant with shiny green foliage, grows from 4 to 6 feet tall and does well in sun or shade; and 'Hetzii', a vigorous plant forming a round mound from 3 to 6 feet tall. 'Compacta' is compact and dense with

glossy foliage; it grows to 3 to 5 feet. 'Convexa' forms a compact 4- to 6-foot mound; leaves are very glossy and cupped downward. 'Helleri', a popular variety, grows very low and dense to 2 to 4 feet tall with dark green leaves. 'Microphylla' is an upright grower reaching 4 to 6 feet with leaves slightly smaller than the species. 'Rotundifolia' grows upright to 6 to 8 feet tall with shiny dark green flat leaves 3/4 to 1-1/4 inches long; it is the largest-leaved variety commonly grown.

Ilex vomitoria
Yaupon
Zones: 7-10. To 15-20 feet.

Yaupon is a small tree or large shrub known for its ability to withstand alkaline soils. Has small dark green leaves. Tiny red berries are produced abundantly without a pollinator. Withstands shearing. 'Nana', the dwarf yaupon, is a mounded shrub to 18 inches high and makes an effective low hedge.

Juniperus
Juniper
Junipers form a large genus of evergreen trees or shrubs containing about 70 species. They produce two kinds of foliage—juvenile and adult. Young plants form sharp short needlelike leaves that clasp the stems. As the plant matures, its new growth produces scalelike foliage that hugs the twigs. Juvenile foliage may continue to be formed on some plants for years. Other forms never produce adult foliage. The color of juniper foliage varies greatly, ranging from all shades of green through blue and gray. Some needles have white undersides.

Junipers can be found for most landscape situations. There are prostrate forms perfect for ground covers and edgings. Others are shrubs that fit into foundation plantings, shrub borders, group plantings, and low hedges. Some species grow into sizeable trees useful as specimen plants, screens, or tall hedges.

Junipers may be pruned lightly to keep their shape symmetrical or sheared heavily for formal hedges or topiary.

Junipers will grow almost anywhere in the United States. They grow in acid or alkaline soils and tolerate hot, dry climates. Best growth is made on dry, sandy, or gravelly soils. Sites must be well drained. A sunny location is best, though in hot areas light shade is acceptable. Plants growing in dense shade or on poorly drained sites are subject to root rot.

Juniper blight, frequently a problem in eastern states, is characterized by browning of branch tips and is encouraged by moist conditions common when plants are watered by overhead sprinklers. The following descriptions include information about disease resistance.

Juniperus chinensis
Chinese Juniper
Zones: 4-10. To 2-75 feet.

Chinese juniper is a variable species. Some types are treelike, some grow as shrubs, and some are ground covers. Leaves range from awl-shaped juvenile needles to mature scalelike ones.

There has been much confusion in identifying all the varieties and forms of Chinese juniper. Some of the low, spreading types, such as pfitzer juniper, are listed under the technical name of *Juniperus x media* and may be sold as cultivars of *J. x media*, although most nurseries do have them listed as cultivars of *J. chinensis*.

'Blue Point' is a pyramidal to columnar shrub with blue-gray foliage. Grows to 8 feet tall.

'Blue Vase' is a vase-shaped juniper with steel-blue foliage, good in summer and winter. An intermediate form between upright and spreading, it can be sheared to keep it small and compact.

'Pfitzerana' is an open shrub to 6 feet high with a spread to 15 feet. Fast-growing, it can quickly become too large for a small garden.

'Pfitzerana Aurea' grows more slowly than 'Pfitzerana'. Its golden-tipped foliage becomes yellowish green in winter.

Many varieties of juniper *(Juniperus sp.)* make excellent ground covers. Their fine-textured foliage combines well with other plants.

Gold coast juniper *(Juniperus chinensis aurea* 'Gold Coast') is a slow-growing, ground-hugging plant with gold tips on the fine foliage.

Blue rug juniper *(Juniper horizontalis 'Wiltonii')* makes a low-maintenance ground cover in place of a lawn.

Junipers *(Juniperus sp.)* are valuable for many landscape uses. They have fine-textured foliage and varied growth habit.

'Pfitzerana Compacta' forms a compact, flat-topped shrub 2 feet high with a spread of 6 feet.

'Pfitzerana Compacta Gold' is a compact form. Its new foliage is golden-yellow.

'San Jose' is low-growing with branches spreading irregularly in all directions. Foliage is sage-green. Grows to 2 feet in height with a 6-foot spread. Can be grown in a container, used in bonsai, set in beds, or used as a ground cover.

'Sea Spray' is a low, compact shrub growing to 1 foot high with a spread of 7 feet. Foliage consists of small blue-green needles. Used mainly as a ground cover.

'Nana' is denser and grows tighter to the ground than most other cultivars. Its leaves are whitish green with a green midrib. Grows to 1 foot high with a spread of 5 feet.

'Variegata' has gray-green foliage highlighted with white. Spreads to 10 feet with 2-foot height. Not as hardy as other varieties, it grows into Zone 6.

J. chinensis procumbens, the Japanese garden juniper, is often sold as *J. procumbens.* This trailing variety has stiff, stout main branches that hug the ground and spread to 21 feet, making it an excellent ground cover for banks.

The variety *J. chinensis sargentii* is sometimes listed as *J. sargentii.* Forms a creeping shrub to 2-1/2 feet high. May spread to 12 feet. Has light green densely packed foliage. Resistant to juniper blight. Cultivars of *sargentii* include 'Glauca', which has a bluish color, and 'Viridis', which has light green foliage.

Variety *J. chinensis aurea* 'Gold Coast™' has gold-tipped foliage. Has a moderate growth rate and compact form.

Juniperus conferta
Shore Juniper
Zones: 6-10. To 2 feet high.

One of the best juniper ground covers, this species from Japan forms a dense, prostrate mat spreading to 15 feet. Originally native along the seashore, it is a good plant for coastal gardens. Bright blue-green leaves are sharp-pointed and prickly to the touch. Use in mass plantings on banks, in planter boxes, and in rock gardens.

'Emerald Sea' makes a low ground-hugging mat; grows to 1 foot high with a spread of 8 feet. 'Blue Pacific' is a slow-growing plant featuring blue-green foliage; grows to 1 foot high with a spread of 8 feet.

Juniperus horizontalis
Creeping Juniper
Zones: 3-7. To 2 feet high.

Creeping juniper has long ropy branches that root as they spread, forming dense mats. It makes an excellent ground cover. Can spread as wide as 8 feet.

Some varieties of creeping juniper grow slowly for the first few years after planting so it won't give you a quick ground cover. A 30-year-old plant can be 2 feet high with a 5-foot spread.

A great many varieties and forms have been developed, some barely distinguishable from each other. Most of these will root along creeping stems, thereby adding almost indefinitely to their diameter or spread.

'Wiltonii', Wilton juniper, is one of the best of the ground cover junipers. It is also sold as 'Blue Rug', 'Blue Wilton', and 'Wilton Carpet Juniper'. It can grow as high as 8 inches by overlapping branches and spread to 10 feet or more. Besides being an ideal ground cover, it is effective planted to drape over the edge of a wall. It is hardy to Zone 4.

'Plumosa', the andorra juniper, has foliage that turns purplish plum in winter. It is 2 feet high and spreads very slowly to 12 feet. Newer selections of 'Plumosa' include 'Plumosa Compacta' with a fuller, more compact habit and 'Plumosa Compacta Youngstown' with a more dense center than other selections.

'Emerald Spreader™' is a new selection that does not mound as some carpet-type junipers do; grows to 1 foot high and 6 feet wide. 'Bar Harbor' is a widely used carpet-type juniper; foliage is plum colored in winter, silver-blue the rest of the year; grows 1 foot high and 10 feet wide.

Juniperus sabina
Savin Juniper
Zones: 3-10. To 15 feet.

Savin juniper is a species of spreading juniper from the mountains of Europe and western Asia. It spreads to 10 feet. The foliage is dark green and has a disagreeable pungent odor when crushed. Grows slowly. After 20 years, a plant may be only 5 feet high with a spread of 7 feet.

'Arcadia', like some other savin junipers, builds itself up by layered branches. It has a height of about 18 inches and an ultimate spread of nearly 10 feet. Features fine-textured bright green foliage. Resistant to juniper blight. 'Calgary Carpet' is a selection of 'Arcadia', having a lower growth habit; grows 1 foot high with a spread of 6 feet.

'Blue Danube' forms a low shrub with greenish-blue foliage on wide-spreading branches. Grows to 2 feet high with a spread of 3 to 12 feet.

'Broadmoor' has gray-green foliage. Grows 1 foot tall with a spread of 4 feet. This dwarf plant is also resistant to juniper blight.

'Buffalo' has feathery branches with bright green foliage and spreads to 8 feet. Stays low, about 1 foot high. Resists juniper blight.

'Savin Variegata' is fast-growing to 3 feet in height with a spread of 5 feet. Lacy branches carry deep green foliage with yellow splashes.

'Scandia' has dark green foliage and grows 18 inches high with a spread of 3 feet. Resistant to juniper blight.

'Tamariscifolia' has long been a popular garden shrub. Mainly used as a ground cover, it grows to 3 feet high with spreads to 20 feet. Covers a bank or wall well. Unfortunately, some varieties are susceptible to juniper blight, which can kill the plant. A new cultivar, 'Tamariscifolia No Blight', is a superior strain that withstands blight better than regular selections.

Hardy tam juniper (*Juniperus sabina* 'Tamariscifolia') is excellent for mass planting on slopes and steep banks.

Dwarf Japanese garden juniper (*Juniperus chinensis procumbens* 'Nana') will cascade over a wall.

Leucothoe *(Leucothoe sp.)* grows in sun or shade. Clusters of white flowers are borne in early spring.

Privet *(Ligustrum sp.)* withstands heavy pruning. Used for hedges, screens, and background plantings.

Leucothoe

Leucothoe, Fetterbush

This genus contains about 50 species of evergreen and deciduous shrubs native to North and South America and Asia. They require moist, well-drained, slightly acid soil rich in organic matter, and will grow in sun or shade. Use in foundation plantings, mass plantings on banks, and as ground covers.

Leucothoe axillaris
Coast Leucothoe
Zones: 6-9. To 6 feet.
Flowering.

This evergreen grows naturally in damp woods, swampy thickets, and along stream banks in the Coastal Plain. Bears white flowers in spring. 'Scarletta', a hybrid of *L. axillaris* and *L. fontanesiana*, grows compactly to 2 feet and has bright red new growth.

Leucothoe fontanesiana
Drooping Leucothoe
Zones: 5-8. To 6 feet.
Flowering.

Drooping leucothoe features long, arching stems heavy with dark green leaves to 7 inches long. Evergreen in the South and semievergreen in the North. Stems are used as cut sprigs by florists. Bears pendulous clusters of white waxy flowers in spring. Leaves turn bronze in fall. Spreads by underground stems. Can be kept pruned to 18 inches and used as a ground cover. 'Girard's Rainbow' has red stems and green leaves marked by yellow.

Ligustrum

Privet

Privets are easily propagated and grow rapidly, making them one of the least expensive hedge plants.

White or cream-colored flowers appear in clusters at stem tips in summer. Some are fragrant; others have an unpleasant aroma. Berries are black or dark blue.

Tough plants, privets can withstand heavy pruning or shearing, which makes them ideal for hedges. Do best in sunny locations but can tolerate shade and city environments. Adapt to a wide range of soils. Dry sites are acceptable although best growth is on moist, fertile soils.

Although a major landscape use for privets is hedges and screens, they are also effective in foundation, border, and background plantings.

Ligustrum japonicum
Japanese Privet
Zones: 7-10. To 10 feet.
Flowering.

This large shrub can be developed into a small tree by pruning. It is easily shaped into topiary forms such as globes and pyramids. Dark green glossy leaves and showy white fragrant flowers make it an ideal specimen plant.

The variety *rotundifolium*, curly leaf privet, is a compact plant with small rounded leaves; it may grow to 6 feet tall. 'Texanum' grows shorter than the species with denser foliage. 'Variegatum' has leaves edged with white.

Ligustrum lucidum
Glossy Privet
Zones: 8-9. To 20-40 feet.
Flowering.

One of the largest privets, glossy privet can be kept at shrub size if pruned. Glossy leaves are 4 to 6 inches long. It makes an attractive specimen all summer with its large, feathery clusters of creamy-white flowers. Can be grown where root space is restricted, even in large containers. Will tolerate salt winds and coastal conditions.

Mahonia

Mahonia

These are evergreen shrubs with bold-textured, shiny, compound leaves with spiny margins. Clusters or spikes of yellow flowers in spring are followed by blue-black berries that are relished by birds. Taller species are useful as textural contrast plants, while lower-growing species are good ground covers or low barrier plants.

Mahonia aquifolium
Oregon Grape
Zones: 5-9. To 2-6 feet.
Flowering.

Upright stems grow from spreading underground stems, forming large patches in its native British Columbia to Northern California. A good plant wherever low masses of evergreen foliage are needed. Leaves are 4 to 10 inches long with 5 to 9 spiny-margined oval leaflets 1 to 2-1/2 inches long. The upper surface is glossy or dull depending on the variety. New growth is often coppery. Winter foliage turns maroon, especially in cold winter areas. 'Compacta' makes a tidy, uniform 2-foot-high planting.

Grows in sun or shade in cool areas. Best in shade in warm areas. Tolerates acid or slightly alkaline soils. Prune to the ground to thicken the stand.

Mahonia bealei
Leatherleaf Mahonia
Zones: 5-10. To 10-12 feet.
Flowering.

The strong vertical stems and horizontal 12- to 16-inch-long compound leaves of this Chinese native make a striking contrast to other plants in the landscape. There are 7 to 15 thick leathery leaflets 2 to 4-1/2 inches long, with 2 to 5 large spines on each side. The leaves are dull bluish green on top, and gray-green below.

Leatherleaf mahonia is a shade plant except in cool coastal areas where it can be grown in full sun. Soil should be moist and contain plenty of organic matter.

Mahonia lomariifolia
Chinese Holly-Grape
Zones: 8-10. To 6-10 feet.
Flowering.

This is a dramatic plant with long, deeply divided, dark green leaves

Oregon grape *(Mahonia aquifolium)* is handsome year-round. Bright yellow flowers in spring precede steel-blue berries (shown below). Winter cold turns foliage maroon.

39

Myoporum *(Myoporum laetum 'Carsonii')* grows rapidly, even in adverse coastal conditions.

Heavenly bamboo *(Nandina domestica)* lends an open airy feeling and changing foliage color to the landscape.

that have spines. They are arranged horizontally around upright stems and may be more than 24 inches long.

An excellent accent plant for entryways, patios, or container growing. Best in partial shade. Prune to induce branching.

Murraya paniculata
Orange Jessamine
Zone: 9. To 5-15 feet.
Flowering.

White flowers with a jasmine-like fragrance and deep green divided leaves on gracefully arching stems make orange jessamine a top-rated shrub. Blooms from late summer into fall. Grows best in filtered shade and with regular watering and fertilizing. Can be pruned as a hedge.

Myoporum laetum 'Carsonii'
Myoporum
Zones: 8-10. To 15-20 feet.
Flowering.

This fast-growing evergreen shrub is greatly appreciated in coastal areas. Features shiny dark green leaves, small white flowers that are not particularly showy, and reddish-purple fruit. If watered regularly, will stand up to blowing sand, wind, and salty air. Grows best in full sun.

Myrtus communis
True Myrtle
Zones: 9-10. To 5-10 feet.
Flowering.

A top-rated hedge plant with small lustrous green leaves, fragrant white flowers, and purplish-black fruit. Grows best in a well-drained soil in shade or hot sun. Tolerates drought. There are several varieties. 'Compacta' is extremely dense with small leaves. 'Microphylla' has small overlapping leaves.

Nandina domestica
Heavenly Bamboo
Zones: 6-10. To 3-8 feet.
Flowering.

Nandina is a many-faceted shrub used to create a mood, spot of color, or interesting textural effect. Slender vertical stems 3 to 8 feet high hold open, delicate foliage. The effect suggests bamboo, although they are not related. Nandina is often used for an Oriental feeling in gardens. New leaves are tinted a bronzy-pink, later soft green, and with winter's cold change to dramatic shades of crimson and purple. Nandina's white flower clusters appear in July, followed by bright red berries that last for several months.

Heavenly bamboo is considered one of the most versatile shrubs for sun or shade, suitable for planting in narrow spaces, containers, borders, and at foundations. Plant shrubs in groupings for cross-pollination and more berry production.

Does well in crowded conditions and accepts almost any soil, although alkaline conditions can cause the shrub to become chlorotic due to iron deficiency. Resistant to oak root fungus and free of pests, nandina is also fairly drought-tolerant once established. In areas where temperatures reach below 0°F, treat it as a herbaceous perennial. Leaves are deciduous at 10°F. Remove all weak shoots to increase density.

'Alba' is a white-berried variety. 'Nana' grows to only 12 to 18 inches high. 'Compacta' is also restrained, but reaches 4 to 5 feet.

Nerium oleander
Oleander
Zones: 8-10. To 8-12 feet.
Flowering.

One of the most widely used evergreen shrubs in California and Arizona, oleander is valued for its colorful display of late spring and summer flowers. Flowers are single or double and are shades of white, yellow, pink, and red. All parts of the plant are poisonous if eaten.

Tolerates heat, drought, poor soils, and wind. Plant in full sun. Shearing seed capsules after flowering will keep plants looking clean. Use as a screen, border or background shrub.

Osmanthus heterophyllus
Holly Olive
Zones: 7-10. To 10 feet.
Flowering.

Osmanthus has long been a garden favorite, admired for its spiny-edged lustrous green foliage and shapely form. Inconspicuous, yet highly fragrant clusters of small creamy-white flowers appear in early fall. Bluish-black berries follow.

Holly olive is an easy-to-grow pest-free plant adaptable to almost any garden soil. Grows in partial shade or full sun. Shapely as an untrimmed or clipped hedge, holly olive is an excellent choice for an informal screen or in foundation or border plantings.

'Gulftide' is an excellent well-branched variety with a compact form growing to 5 to 8 feet. 'Purpureus' adds color to the garden with dark purple young leaves that remain tinted through the summer. 'Rotundifolius' makes a handsome slow-growing shrub to 5 feet. Its leaves are rounded rather than holly-like. 'Variegatus' will add sparkle to shaded areas with its white-margined leaves. Grows slowly to form a dense 5-foot shrub.

Photinia x fraseri
Red-Tip Photinia
Zones: 7-10. To 10 feet.
Flowering.

The bright bronzy-red new leaves of photinia are as colorful a display in early spring as the blossoms of any flowering shrub. Large flat-headed clusters of white flowers follow new growth in March and April. Red berries follow, adding to the visual interest. Photinia responds well to pruning for a controlled shape, formal hedge, or

Red-tip photinia *(Photonia x fraseri)* has brilliant bronzy-red new foliage; showy white flowers in spring followed by red berries. Withstands pruning.

Holly olive *(Osmanthus heterophyllus)*

Bird's nest spruce (Picea abies 'Nidiformis') is very cold hardy. May spread to 6 feet, grow 3 feet tall.

Lily-of-the-valley shrub (Pieris japonica) produces pendulous clusters of white blossoms in spring. (Above.) Young leaves may be bronze. (Below.)

espalier. Useful as an unpruned screen or background plant.

Photinia readily accepts high heat and sun if watered regularly, or drier conditions in partial shade. Aphids and scale are occasional problems.

Picea

Spruce

Spruce are normally tall, symmetrical trees with stiff whorls of branches and short, sharp needles that are arranged in whorls around the branches. They are very cold hardy. Several dwarf forms make intriguing shrubs for specimen plants in rock gardens, shrub borders, or beside entryways. Needs full sun and adapts to most soils as long as there is adequate moisture.

Picea abies
Norway Spruce
Zones: 2-8. To 6 feet.

'Nidiformis' is called the bird's-nest spruce because its dense branches form a globe with a depression on top. It is an unusual form, suitable for rock gardens; grows to 3 feet tall and 6 feet wide. 'Clanbrassiliana' is a globular shrub with very dense branches; grows very slowly to 6 feet tall and 10 feet wide. 'Pendula' makes a good ground cover, growing 1-1/2 feet tall and eventually spreading to 10 feet wide.

Picea glauca albertiana
Alberta Spruce
Zones: 2-5. To 7 feet.

This graceful, soft-textured conifer bears little resemblance to the giant spruce trees. It is a dwarf form with very tiny, soft needles colored grass-green. Grows slowly into a neat 7-foot-tall cone.

Pieris

Andromeda, Pieris

Pieris are ornamental plants grown for their foliage and clusters of white or pink flowers in spring. They can be used as specimens in groupings with other evergreen plants, as well as in naturalistic plantings. Do not crowd, but allow shrubs room for development.

A moist, acid, well-drained soil is required. Grows best in partial shade. Light shade afforded by tall scattered trees is ideal. Some sun for short periods aids flower formation.

Pieris floribunda
Fetterbush, Mountain Andromeda
Zones: 5-9. To 6 feet.
Flowering.

This dense shrub is the hardiest of the pieris. Bears upright pyramidal clusters of white flowers in early spring.

'Karenoma' is a fast-growing compact shrub with snow-white flowers in early spring.

Pieris japonica
Andromeda, Japanese Pieris, Lily-of-the-Valley Shrub
Zones: 5-9. To 9-10 feet.
Flowering.

An upright-growing shrub with stiff, spreading branches, Japanese pieris bears pendulous clusters of white flowers very early in spring. New growth is bronze, changing to dark green as leaves develop. Dislikes strong winds and grows best on protected sites in Zone 5. Many cultivars have been selected.

Pinus

Pine

Most pines are tall, evergreen trees admired for their graceful shape and elegant clusters of needles. One, *P. mugo*, is naturally dwarf and makes an excellent slow-growing shrub. Of the popular landscape trees, many pines have dwarf, spreading, or mounding forms that can be used as shrubs.

Pines need full sun and adapt to most soil conditions.

Pinus mugo
Mugo Pine
Zones: 2-8. To 1-6 feet.

Mugo pines are compact plants with dense clusters of bright green needles. They usually form a rounded mound that is wider than tall.

P. mugo mugo is the standard mugo pine. It grows slowly to 6 feet and has an irregular shape. The variety *pumilio* grows only an inch a year and forms a spreading 5-foot mound. 'Gnome' reaches an ultimate height of 14 inches and has very dark green needles.

Pinus strobus 'Nana'
Dwarf White Pine
Zones: 2-8. To 3-7 feet.

This low-spreading pine forms a dense soft-looking mound of feathery blue-green needles. Makes a good plant for an accent beside an entryway, in a rock garden, or in a low border.

Pinus sylvestris 'Nana'
Dwarf Scotch Pine
Zones: 3-8. To 4-6 feet.

Twisted bluish-green needles on horizontal or slightly weeping branches give this dwarf shrub a rugged character. Forms a dense, rounded bush.

Pittosporum tobira
Mock Orange, Tobira
Zones: 8-10. To 6-15 feet. Flowering.

Lustrous leaves, fragrant flowers, and low maintenance are responsible for the popularity of tobira. It is an excellent foundation, specimen, or screening plant. Grows well in containers.

Tobira is a medium-sized shrub of vigorous growth, and broad, upright habit, with heavy branches. Leaves are spaced so close together on the stems that they appear to be in whorls, giving the plant a very solid appearance. Leathery and glossy dark green leaves. Small creamy-white five-petaled flowers, borne in spring, have the scent of orange blossoms. Small pear-shaped seed capsules split in fall, showing orange seeds.

Plant in sun or semishade. Although fairly drought-resistant,

Mugo pines *(Pinus mugo)* are hardy and adaptable. Their soft mounded form makes them an attractive ground cover, specimen, or accent plant.

Tobira *(Pittosporum tobira)* grows vigorously, and has dense foliage, making it a good screening plant. Produces flowers scented like orange blossoms in spring.

The white-rimmed leaves of variegated tobira (*Pittosporum tobira* 'Variegata') make a bright landscape display.

Golden Oriental arborvitae (*Platycladus orientalis* 'Aureus Nanus') is soft-textured, has yellow tips on summer foliage.

appearance is enhanced with moderate watering. Aphids and scale are major insect problems.

'Variegata' has attractive gray-green leaves edged with white; not as vigorous as the species, reaching an ultimate height of only 5 feet. 'Wheeler's Dwarf' is a very low 1- to 2-foot, compact mounding plant with dense, whorled foliage.

Platycladus orientalis

Oriental Arborvitae

Zones: 6-10. To 30 feet.

Botanists have had a difficult time deciding which genus this plant belongs to. It has been classified as *Thuja*, *Biota*, and finally *Platycladus*. Oriental arborvitae is sold under all three names.

It is normally a large rounded shrub, or small conical tree, frequently multistemmed. Although the foliage is normally scalelike in flat sprays, a few cultivars retain the needlelike or awl-shaped juvenile foliage and do not resemble the typical plants.

Arborvitae is tolerant of most soils that have good drainage and ample moisture. Avoid locations where there is reflected heat from light-colored surfaces of buildings and pavement. Landscape uses include foundation, group, and border plantings; use as specimens, and in formal rows.

'Aureus Nanus' is a globose densely foliaged plant growing 5 to 8 feet tall; green foliage tipped with yellow in summer becomes somewhat bronzed in winter. 'Texanus Glaucus' is a pyramid-shaped plant with blue juvenile foliage. 'Raffles' is a dense globe-shaped dwarf with golden foliage; grows to 5 feet tall. 'Bakeri', a compact pyramidal plant with pale green foliage, grows 10 to 25 feet tall; hardier than most other cultivars, it is adapted to hot, dry localities. 'Blue Cone' is a pyramidal upright plant hardy to Zone 5; foliage becomes brown at −17°F, but the plant recovers; may reach 9 feet.

Prunus

Flowering Fruit, Prunus

Two species of this large family of deciduous and evergreen plants are top-rated evergreen shrubs.

Prunus caroliniana
Carolina Cherry Laurel
Zones: 7-10. To 20-40 feet.
Flowering.

A large evergreen shrub or small tree, this fast-growing species is top-rated for a large screen or clipped hedge.

Leaves are deep glossy green, 2 to 4 inches long, and have smooth edges. New foliage is bronze colored when emerging. Small creamy-white flowers in 1-inch spikes open between February and April. Black fruits, 1/2 inch or less in diameter, last into winter if birds don't eat them. Falling fruit can be messy.

The variety 'Compacta' is slow-growing and compact. 'Bright 'n Tight' is also small and compact. Both make excellent hedges.

Carolina cherry laurel grows well in average soil but will show chlorosis and leaf burn in alkaline soils. Shrubs grow best in cool, moist coastal areas, but they can take full sun and high heat. Established plants are drought-tolerant.

Prunus laurocerasus
English Laurel
Zones: 7-10. To 5-30 feet.
Flowering.

In mild climates, this rapidly growing shrub can easily reach 30 feet tall and wide. In cold areas growth will be restrained. Makes a very effective screen or clipped hedge, although the fast growth calls for frequent clipping.

Glossy dark-green oval leaves are 3 to 7 inches long. Small fragrant white flowers stand above the foliage in long clusters. They are followed by small black fruits. 'Otto Luyken' is a low-growing variety.

Takes full sun in cool climates. Grow in partial shade in hot areas. Roots are invasive.

Pyracantha
Firethorn

Six species of evergreen or deciduous, usually thorny shrubs are contained in this genus. They are used as ornamental specimen plants, in barrier hedges, and as espaliers. When trained as espaliers, firethorns can reach twice the height they achieve as shrubs.

Flat clusters of petite flowers add visual impact in spring. The real display of color begins in late summer or early autumn when the masses of berries turn red to orange; they persist into winter.

Firethorns do not do well in acid soils. A sunny location is preferred. Evergreen in mild climates, leaves may be deciduous in cold northern areas.

In some areas, certain pyracantha varieties are subject to fireblight, a bacterial disease that kills branches. They can also be susceptible to apple scab, a fungus that disfigures fruit and foliage. Select disease-resistant cultivars rather than bothering with control measures. Recently developed disease-resistant hybrids include: 'Fiery Cascade', which grows to 8 feet tall; 'Mohave', which grows to 12 feet tall; 'Rutgers', which grows to 3 feet tall and spreads to 9 feet; and 'Teton', which reaches 15 feet high. All are adapted to Zones 6 to 9.

Pyracantha angustifolia
Narrowleaf Firethorn
Zones: 5-9. To 12 feet.
Flowering.

This species can be either upright or prostrate. Leaves are narrow to 2 inches long. White flowers are bunched in clusters to 1-1 2 inches wide. Bright orange to brick-red fruits are retained through winter. The species is only hardy to Zone 7.

The cultivar 'Gnome' is hardier than the species and can grow in Zone 5. It is half the height of the species with a compact, densely branched growth habit.

English laurel *(Prunus laurocerasus)* forms a dense hedge or shrub very quickly. Bears fragrant white flowers in late spring.

Firethorn *(Pyracantha sp.)* can be grown as a cascading shrub or as an espalier.

45

Firethorn berries (Pyracantha sp.) add brilliant color to the fall and winter landscape.

Indian hawthorn (Raphiolepis indica) blooms profusely from midwinter into spring and again in autumn.

Pyracantha coccinea
Scarlet Firethorn
Zones: 5-9. To 6 feet.
Flowering.

This species, covered with bright red fruits in autumn, drops its leaves in colder regions. Usually one of its many cultivars are selected for garden use. The species is only hardy to Zone 7.

The cultivar 'Lalandei' is hardier than the species, growing into Zone 5; grows vigorously to 10 feet; orange-red berries are borne during fall. It is resistant to fireblight. 'Kasan' is also hardier than the species and is one of the most cold-tolerant of all scarlet firethorn cultivars; bright orange-red berries are held well into the winter.

'Colorado Red' is hardy into Zone 5. A vigorous-growing plant with bright red berries.

Pyracantha koidzumii
Formosa Firethorn
Zones: 7-10. To 10 feet.
Flowering.

This densely branched shrub with abundant small orange-red to dark red berries spreads to 8 feet. 'Santa Cruz Prostrata' is a cultivar forming a prostrate shrub and bearing masses of red berries in autumn.

Pyracantha 'Tiny Tim'
Tiny Tim Firethorn
Zones: 7-9. To 3 feet.
Flowering.

This dwarf is nearly thornless, with cinnamon-red fruits. Useful in borders, foundations, or patio planters.

Raphiolepis indica
Indian Hawthorn
Zones: 8-10. To 2-5 feet.
Flowering.

Showy flowers and a hardy nature have established Indian hawthorn as one of the finest top-rated shrubs. Handsome leathery foliage is a deep green, and is often bronze or red when young. From midwinter through spring, and again in fall, a profusion of tiny flowers appears. Varieties are available with white, pink, or deep rose-red blossoms, and a choice of forms.

Bluish-black berries are held through winter.

Indian hawthorn has become popular for use as a ground cover, informal hedge, colorful accent, foundation shrub, or container plant. This shrub is adaptable to a wide range of soils. Fairly drought-tolerant, it thrives with regular watering. In full sun, it will bloom prolifically but is also suitable for partly shaded exposures. Leaf spot, aphids, and fireblight are occasional problems.

Rhododendron
Rhododendron, Azalea

There are over 900 species and more than 10,000 named varieties in the genus *Rhododendron*, which includes all the plants once placed in the genus *Azalea*. They are native to many parts of the world including North America. Rhododendrons are generally large, leathery-leaved plants bearing bold clusters of flowers at the branch tips. Azaleas usually have small leaves and are covered with masses of flowers in spring.

Azalea flowers may be single, semidouble, double, or hose-in-hose. Double blossoms result from stamens becoming petal-like. Hose-in-hose flowers are formed when the sepals (the green "leaves" at the bases of the flowers) become petal-like. Hose-in-hose flowers may be single, double, and semidouble. Rhododendron flowers are single or more commonly in trusses.

Rhododendrons and azaleas require a fertile acid soil that drains rapidly. If drainage is questionable, plant above ground in either raised beds or mounds. Add organic matter such as peat moss, ground bark, or compost to heavy soils to improve drainage.

Many varieties may be grown with great success in containers. A soil mix of 50 percent peat moss and 50 percent sand or perlite is ideal.

Water rhododendrons and azaleas regularly and fertilize with acid fertilizer. Most varieties do best in partial shade. Protect plants from wind.

Rhododendron hybrids
Evergreen Azaleas
Zones: 6-10.
Flowering.

Botanists have organized the genus *Rhododendron* into series and subseries, and azaleas are one of the prime series. Azaleas are further categorized into groups of hybrids with special characteristics; each group has its own named varieties in a wide range of flower types and colors. The evergreen groups listed here are in order of least to most cold hardy.

Belgian Indica: Large double or semidouble flowers; hardy to 20° to 30°F, Zones 8-10. **Rutherfordiana:** Single, semidouble, or double blossoms of medium size; hardy to 20° to 30°F, Zones 8-10. **Southern Indica:** Small to medium single blossoms; hardy to 20°F, Zones 8-10. **Satsuki:** Single or double blooms; hardy to 5° to 10°F, Zones 7-10. **Kurume:** Masses of small flowers; hardy to 5° to 10°F, Zones 7-10. **Macrantha:** Large single to hose-in-hose flowers; hardy to 5°F, Zones 7-10. **Pericat:** Large flowers; hardy to 5° to 10°F, Zones 7-10. **Gable Hybrids:** Medium-sized hose-in-hose blossoms; hardy to 0°F, Zones 7-8. **Glenn Dale Hybrids:** Wide variety of flower types and sizes; hardy to 0° to 10°F, Zones 7-8. **Kaempferi Hybrids:** Flowers include a color range of orange and red; hardy to −15°F, Zones 5-8.

Rhododendron hybrids
Rhododendrons
Zones: 4-9.
Flowering.

Rhododendrons are among the most important evergreen shrubs in northern gardens. Many take subzero winters in stride, then cover themselves with magnificent flowers in spring.

Many rhododendrons have big, bold-textured leaves and the plants become massive. Compact or dwarf

The luxuriant foliage of evergreen azaleas *(Rhododendron sp.)* is handsome year-round; may turn bronze or red in fall and winter. Brilliant spring blooms are a colorful spectacle.

'Anah Kruschke' rhododendron *(Rhododendron sp.)*

Japanese skimmia *(Skimmia japonica)* serves many landscape uses. Fragrant ivory-white flowers are followed by red fruit, shown below.

varieties are best for small properties. The following rhododendrons are the most popular according to a recent poll of 20 chapters of the American Rhododendron Society from many different geographic regions.

'Anah Kruschke': Flowers lavender-blue to reddish purple; hardy to −10°F, Zones 6-9. **'Anna Rose Whitney':** Flowers large, rose-pink; hardy to −5°F, Zones 6-9. **'Antoon van Welie':** Flowers deep pink; hardy to −5°F, Zones 6-9. **'Boule de Neige':** Flowers white; hardy to −25°F, Zones 4-9. **'Bow Bells':** Rounded, spreading, to 3 feet tall, flowers light pink; hardy to 0°F, Zones 6-9. **'Caroline':** Flowers orchid-pink; hardy to −15°F, Zones 5-9. **'Dora Amateis':** Semidwarf, spice-scented flowers are pure white; hardy to −15°F, Zones 5-9. **'Fragrantissimum':** Flowers white tinged pink; fragrant; hardy to 20°F, Zones 9-10. **'Janet Blair':** Flowers light pink; hardy to −15°F, Zones 5-9. **'The Hon. Jean Marie de Montague':** Flowers bright red; hardy to 0°F, Zones 6-9. **'Mrs. Furnival':** Spreading, to 4 feet in height, flowers light pink; hardy to −10°F, Zones 6-9. **'Nova Zembla':** Flowers dark red; hardy to −25°F, Zones 4-9. **'P.J.M.':** Compact, small-leaved, flowers lavender-pink; hardy to −20°F, Zones 5-9. **'Roseum Elegans':** Flowers rose-lilac; hardy to −25°F, Zones 4-9. **'Scintillation':** Flowers pastel-pink; hardy to −10°F, Zones 6-9. **'Unique':** Grows to 4 feet in height, flowers light cream-yellow; hardy to 0°F, Zones 6-9. **'Windbeam':** Small aromatic foliage, grows to 4 feet in height, flowers white to light pink; hardy to −25°F, Zones 4-9.

Complete descriptions of rhododendron and azalea varieties and species can be found in *Top-Rated Azaleas and Rhododendrons,* another book in this series.

Rosmarinus officinalis
Rosemary
Zones: 7-10. To 2-6 feet.
Flowering.

This dense-branching shrub has aromatic leaves that are narrow, glossy dark green and grayish white on the undersides. Bears small light-blue flowers in winter and spring.

Rosemary has been grown in herb gardens since ancient times. It is now also commonly used for hedges, especially in Southern California. Low-growing and prostrate forms are used as ground covers on dry rocky sites. Also good in coastal regions. In cold climates, plant in containers and move indoors during freezing weather.

Sarcococca hookerana humilis
Sweet Box
Zones: 7-10. To 15-24 inches.
Flowering.

Sweet box is a slow-growing, handsomely formed plant, which spreads by underground runners to 8 feet wide. Glossy green lance-shaped leaves hide the tiny, fragrant white flowers in early spring. Small shiny black berries follow in summer. This plant's greatest asset is its tolerance of deep shade. It is a valuable shrub for north-facing exposures, entryways, and for greenery under tall shrubs. It forms a lush ground cover.

Sweet box is an easy-to-grow shrub demanding little attention. Plant in a rich, well-drained soil with plenty of organic matter added. Water regularly. Watch for signs of scale.

Skimmia japonica
Japanese Skimmia
Zones: 6-8. To 5 feet.
Flowering.

Japanese skimmia is a handsome plant grown for its fragrant flowers, attractive fruits, and bright green foliage. Flowers are yellowish white, fruits are bright red or bright scarlet and leaves are 3 to 4 inches long. A dome-shaped shrub, it has a dense habit of growth.

Grows best in moist, sandy loam soils but tolerates some clay. Grows in light to full shade. Requires more shade farther south but heavy or dense shade will cause plants to become leggy. Because male and female flowers are usually on different plants both a male and female shrub are required to ensure a set of fruit on the female plant. A number of male and female cultivars have been selected.

Skimmias are tough and will grow in urban areas. They are frequently used in foundation plantings, as specimens, in shady borders, and as container plants.

Taxus
Yew

Yews are slow-growing, densely foliaged shrubs or trees with handsome deep green needles. Female plants form red berries that are poisonous if eaten in large quantities. Since yews come in all shapes and sizes, they are suitable for many landscape situations. Commonly grown as shrubs, they are used in foundation plantings, as hedges or screens, and as individual specimens. They respond very well to shearing. Low-growing forms make good ground covers. The treelike forms can be kept shrublike by pruning.

Yews will grow on most types of soils provided there is good drainage and they are protected from strong winds. They grow in full sun or partial shade.

Taxus baccata
English Yew
Zones: 6-9. To 60 feet.

This is a large species with over 100, mostly European, cultivars. Foliage is a deeper green than the hardier Japanese yew. 'Repandens' is wide spreading, 10 feet high by 30 feet wide. 'Adpressa' is compact and dense and reaches 4 to 5 feet high.

Taxus cuspidata
Japanese Yew
Zones: 5-9. To 65 feet.

This popular landscape shrub has densely foliaged twigs with slender yellow-green needles.

'Capitata' is an upright, pyramidal form; pruning is necessary to keep it symmetrical; often used at

Yews *(Taxus sp.)* withstand shearing and are popular shrubs with a wide range of uses including specimen plants, hedges, screens, and foundation plants. English yew *(Taxus baccata)* foliage shown below.

49

Many varieties of American arborvitae *(Thuja occidentalis)* are top-rated garden plants useful for windbreaks, hedges, foundation plants, or specimen plants. Landscape uses shown above and below.

corners of buildings in foundation plantings. 'Nana' is one of the oldest cultivars of Japanese yew; it is a dense, wide-spreading plant with upright branches that grows very slowly.

Taxus x media
Hybrid Yew
Zones: 5-9. To 40 feet.

A hybrid between English and Japanese yews, this popular shrub has the hardiness of the Japanese parent and the beauty of the English one. Numerous cultivars have been selected. 'Brownii' is a globular plant commonly used for hedges and in foundations. 'Hicksii' is an upright shrub. 'Wardii' is a very common, wide, spreading shrub.

Thuja occidentalis
American Arborvitae, Eastern Arborvitae
Zones: 3-9. To 40-60 feet.

Naturally a tall, conical tree with flat sprays of scalelike leaves, many shrublike forms of this popular evergreen are available. As landscape plants they are commonly used in foundation plantings, as windbreaks, and hedges, and as accent plants. Dwarf varieties are suitable for rock gardens.

Best growth is made in full sunlight although light shade is acceptable. Fertile, moist, well-drained soils produce the most vigorous plants.

'Reingold' is a cone-shaped shrub with golden foliage; grows to 12 feet. 'Woodwardii' holds its globe shape without pruning; has dark green foliage; grows slowly to 8 feet. 'Aurea' is a golden-yellow globe to 3 feet high. 'Canadian Green' has bright green foliage, a globe shape, and grows to 3 feet.

Tsuga canadensis 'Pendula'
Sargent Weeping Hemlock
Zones: 5-9. To 3 feet.

This weeping variety of the graceful Canadian hemlock is a stunning specimen plant for rock gardens, entryways, and shrub borders. The soft, fine-textured needles are dark green with white lines on the undersides. Reaches 3 feet tall and 6 feet wide. Grows best in moist, acid soil. Provide partial shade in areas with hot summer sun.

Viburnum
Viburnum
Viburnums are a diverse group of plants. They can be evergreen or deciduous, grow low or tall, and be cold hardy or tender. Some are grown primarily for their foliage, others for their flowers, and still others for their brightly colored fruit. Many species have more than one outstanding feature.

With few exceptions viburnums tolerate both alkaline and acid soils. They grow well in wet, heavy, fertile soils and some species also tolerate drought. They grow in sun or shade, although evergreen species look better with some shade in hot, dry climates. Evergreen species can be pruned to control size and shape. Many are subject to aphid damage.

Viburnum odoratissimum
Sweet Viburnum
Zones: 7-10. To 10-20 feet.
Flowering.

Sweet viburnum has bright green leaves 3 to 8 inches long and 2 to 4 inches wide with a glossy upper surface. Older leaves often become purplish in winter in cool climates. In colder climates leaves may drop. Lightly fragrant flowers in 3- to 6-inch pyramidal clusters open in May. Red berries turn black when fully ripe. Shrubs are wider than tall.

Viburnum suspensum
Sandankwa Viburnum
Zones: 9-10. To 4-8 feet.
Flowering.

This medium-sized shrub spreads as wide as it is tall. Oval, leathery, glossy dark green leaves are 2 to 4 inches long. Flat loose clusters of rose-tinted white flowers are 2 to 4 inches across. Their fragrance is objectionable to some people. Round red berries ripen to black.

Viburnum tinus
Laurustinus
Zones: 7-10. To 4-10 feet.
Flowering.

This native of the Mediterranean region is one of the rare winter-blooming shrubs. Flowers often open as early as November and last into spring. Dense foliage from top to bottom of the plant makes it good for hedges or screens, and it can be sheared into topiary figures.

Dark, glossy green, oval leaves are 2 to 3 inches long. Tight flat clusters of pink buds open to lightly fragrant white flowers in late fall. Bright metallic-blue berries last through summer.

May develop mildew in cool, moist climates. Withhold water and fertilizer in late summer to prevent frost-sensitive, vigorous growth.

Several varieties of laurustinus are available. 'Dwarf' grows only 3 to 5 feet tall and as wide; use in foundation plantings and for low hedges. 'Robustum', round-leaf laurustinus, has larger leaves and lighter pink flowers than the species; resistant to mildew, it grows in a wide variety of climates. 'Spring Bouquet' has slightly smaller and darker green foliage than the species; its compact upright growth to 6 feet makes it a good hedge plant.

Xylosma congestum (X. senticosum)
Shiny Xylosma
Zones: 8-10. To 4-30 feet.

Growth pattern and uses for this plant vary depending on the pruning and cultural practices. It is a versatile plant that can be used for a hedge, espalier, or even a ground cover. When left unpruned, an open, graceful, wide-spreading shrub 8 to 10 feet tall will develop. The variety 'Compactum' is slower growing and about half the size of xylosma at maturity.

Leaves are 1-1 2 to 2 inches long with rounded bases and long tapering points. They are a beautiful, shiny yellowish green when mature, bronzy-red when new.

Xylosma grows on most soils and is heat- and drought-tolerant. Grows best in full sun or light shade.

Shiny xylosma *(Xylosma congestum)* is a versatile plant that withstands pruning. Bronzy-red new leaves mature to green.

Laurustinus *(Viburnum tinus)* blossoms in winter. Withstands shearing for a hedge, screen or topiary.

Caring for Evergreen Shrubs

Once you have chosen the shrub that suits your landscaping needs, you naturally want it to prosper in your garden. Ensure this by following recommended practices for soil preparation, planting, watering, pruning, and fertilizing.

PREPLANTING CARE

Evergreen shrubs are sold in two forms: balled-and-burlapped and in containers.

Balled-and-burlapped: These shrubs, which are best planted in spring or fall, are dug from the field where they grow and the ball of roots and soil is wrapped in burlap for shipping. Before planting, keep the foliage moist and water the rootball frequently and slowly from the top. Keep the shrub shaded and out of the wind and plant as soon as possible.

When handling balled-and-burlapped plants, be careful to lift them from the bottom; never use the trunk as a handle. If the shrub cannot stand upright, tie it to a fence or wedge it between heavy objects until it's planted.

Container: Most evergreen shrubs available at the nursery are container-grown. They can be purchased and planted anytime. However, if you are shopping for a flowering evergreen shrub, such as a camellia or hibiscus, wait until flowering time to buy. Individual plants, even of the same species, vary, and seeing them in flower is the only way to be sure of getting the flower color and form you want.

When selecting a container-grown plant, don't choose the smallest or largest in the group. If the smallest is small due to weak and slow growth, or whatever the

At left: Variegated tobira *(Pittosporum tobira* 'Variegata') can be clipped into a neat formal hedge with two-handed shears.

Andromeda *(Pieris japonica)*

Firethorn *(Pyracantha sp.)*

cause, this weak growth will most likely continue. The largest shrubs have too much top growth compared to root growth—a low root-to-top ratio. Such plants are more likely to suffer excessive shock after planting.

Containers are usually plastic or metal. Most nursery personnel will offer to cut the sides of metal cans for you. This makes planting easier, but is recommended only if you are sure you can plant the shrub the same day. Once cans are cut, the rootball dries out very quickly. To help slow moisture loss, press the sides of cut containers together and tie with twine.

Most containers, metal or plastic, are dark-colored. When exposed to direct sunlight, the container can quickly heat up to root-damaging levels. Shade the container with a board, mounded soil, or low wall.

Soil

Soil texture, drainage, and acid-alkaline balance, or "pH", are the three basic qualities to consider when planting evergreen shrubs.

Soil texture: The relative quantities of sand, silt, and clay determine your soil's texture. Sandy soils have limited water and nutrient reserves but permit ample amounts of air to circulate around roots. Clay soils, by contrast, have plenty of water and nutrient capacity but restrict air. Loam soils are intermediate between sandy and clay soils and combine the best characteristics of each.

The addition of organic matter, for instance composted bark or sawdust, peat moss, or leafmold, is the best way to improve either clay or sandy soils. In these soils, make planting holes twice as wide as otherwise recommended and refill the hole with amended soil.

Soil drainage: Check drainage before planting by filling the planting hole with water, allowing it to completely drain, filling it again, and then timing how long the water takes to drain. If less than 1/4 inch of water drains after one hour, drainage is too slow. You can improve it by boring through restrictive soil layers with an auger or posthole digger and then filling the drainage hole with amended soil.

Soil pH: Chemists measure soil acidity and alkalinity on the pH scale. The scale ranges from 0 to 14, the numbers below 7 indicating acidity, those above 7 indicating alkalinity. Midpoint, 7, is neutral.

Soil pH generally is determined by the amount of rainfall in an area, though individual gardens in an area may vary slightly. Rain washes natural limestone from soil, increasing its acidity. Areas of high rainfall have the most acid soil, areas of low rainfall the most alkaline soil.

Most evergreen shrubs prefer a slightly acid soil, measuring between 6 and 7 on the pH scale. Some shrubs are referred to as "acid-loving". These include gardenias, camellias, hollies, and azaleas. A few shrubs, such as cotoneaster, prefer a slightly alkaline soil.

You can determine the pH of your garden soil by using one of the simple test kits available at most garden centers, or ask your local county agricultural extension office about soil tests done by universities or private laboratories in your area.

To raise the pH from 5.5 to 6.5, add ground dolomite limestone, 4 to 8 pounds per 100 square feet. Use less in sandy soil, more in clay soil. Limestone is slow acting, so try to add it 1 or 2 months before planting.

Use sulfur, iron sulfate, and organic matter to lower a high pH. Sulfur at 2 pounds per 100 square feet will gradually reduce pH from 7.5 to 6.5. About 4 pounds of iron sulfate per 100 square feet has the same effect. Organic matter of any kind will gradually increase soil acidity as it decomposes.

WHEN TO PLANT

The best time to plant evergreen shrubs is fall, when temperatures are moderate and soil is relatively warm, encouraging root growth. If you live where soil freezes, plant in early fall and mulch after planting. The mulch will moderate temperatures, preventing the alternate freezing and thawing that damages roots of partially established plants.

Spring is the second best planting time. Again, temperatures are moderate, minimizing stress on plants. Summer planting is usually not recommended since high heat, coupled with limited roots, is often enough to kill young plants. However, if you give extra attention to watering, summer planting can be successful.

SPACING

Spacing of shrubs is determined by the specific plant's mature height and spread, as well as its intended use. For instance, if a plant will eventually become 4 feet wide, plant it so the trunk is half that far from the house, fence, or neighboring shrubs. When mature, its branch tips will just slightly reach or overlap those of nearby plants.

Hedge plants are generally spaced between 2 and 4 feet apart. Larger-growing plants for taller hedges should be spaced more widely, plants for very low hedges, more closely. To plant a straight hedge, mark the planting row with stakes and string. Then dig a trench beneath the string. Measure the spacing between shrubs accurately.

THE PLANTING HOLE

Planting techniques vary depending upon whether you are planting a balled-and-burlapped or a container-grown shrub. But for both types, you should start with a hole the same depth and twice the width of the rootball.

If you are planting from containers, or if your garden's soil is heavy clay or very sandy, amend the soil you dug from the hole. Mix two parts soil with organic material such as compost, peat moss, or shredded bark. Firmly pack amended soil in the bottom of the planting hole, water, and then allow to drain. Use amended soil as backfill to refill the hole around the shrub's roots. This 2-to-1 mix provides a transition between the usually lightweight container soil mix and heavier garden soil.

Planting

All evergreen shrubs should be situated in the planting hole so that the new soil level is the same as it was at the nursery or in its container. If necessary, add soil to the bottom of the planting hole until the shrub rests at the proper height. Try the plant in the hole, adjusting it in various directions until the most attractive side faces the most frequent viewpoint.

With a balled-and-burlapped shrub, once most of the backfill is in place, untie the burlap covering and spread it back, burying it as you fill in the hole. The burlap will eventually rot. A plant grown in a wood-fiber container may be left in the container when you plant it. Just tear away the 1 or 2 inches of container that protrudes above soil level.

Soil

Clay soil has a smooth texture and retains moisture.

Sandy soil is gritty, loose, and fast-draining.

Loam soil combines the best features of clay and sandy soils.

Planting

1. Combine organic amendment with garden soil to make backfill mix.

2. Add backfill to planting hole if it is deeper than the rootball.

3. Add water to planting hole to moisten and settle backfill.

4. Loosen roots that the container has forced to coil or circle, and set rootball in planting hole.

5. Add backfill around rootball, firming with your hands as you go.

6. Be sure the original rootball receives ample water the first year after planting.

Pruning after planting: Pruning at this time is especially important for balled-and-burlapped evergreen shrubs. These plants have lost many roots when they were dug from the field. Prune their top growth to compensate for lost roots.

It is a good idea to prune container-grown evergreen shrubs right after planting since a few roots are often damaged during transplanting. In fact, some gardeners recommend purposefully trimming container-plant rootballs to stimulate new root growth away from the circular pattern caused by the shape of the container.

Always remove any dead or broken branches. As necessary, cut away about one-third of young, healthy branches to maintain the plant's attractive, natural proportions. Make cuts just above buds (found where a leaf stem joins a branch) that point in the direction you want subsequent growth to take.

Watering

After planting, make a low basin with loose soil around the plant to hold water. Make the basin slightly larger than the shrub's original balled-and-burlapped or container rootball. It is important—especially at first—for the rootball to be thoroughly soaked with each watering. If the texture of the rootball soil and the garden soil is very different, sometimes the ground can be adequately watered, but the rootball remains dry.

New evergreen shrubs, no matter how drought-tolerant once established, need regular watering during their first season. There are many ways to water efficiently. Ideally the method you use will distribute water uniformly without excessive runoff. The best ways of getting water to plants are basins, furrows, sprinklers, and drip systems.

Basins: A basin is a low dike of earth that holds water around a plant's root area. Established plants need a basin about as wide as the shrub's leafy canopy, or "drip line". Individual basins work well if you have a few shrubs a convenient distance from the hose.

Furrows: These are shallow trenches that direct water flow. Use narrow furrows to connect one shrub's basin to the next, or wider furrows, (12 to 15 inches) to water established shrubs.

Sprinklers: This is probably the most common method of watering. Established shrubs will need less frequent and deeper watering than lawns. Consider using "bubble" sprinkler heads or hose nozzles designed for shrub plantings. Placed inside a basin to confine water, bubblers are an efficient watering method.

Drip watering: There are many varieties of drip watering systems, but most are a combination of small diameter plastic tubing and emitters, small valves that allow the water to drip out. Drip watering systems allow a precise application of water at a rate the soil can absorb. Since soil between plants is not watered, weed growth is not encouraged. Drip watering systems are especially useful for watering plants on slopes and wherever it is otherwise difficult to avoid runoff.

Use enough emitters to completely water the rootball and soil surrounding the shrub. Depending upon the type used, one or two emitters are enough for a small shrub. If you plan to use a drip watering system for shrubs, look for one that can be expanded by adding emitters as shrubs grow and need more water.

Fertilizing

Most evergreen shrubs need very little fertilizing. Needled evergreens may never require fertilizer. If many leaves, especially older leaves in full sun, become yellow, nitrogen fertilizer may be needed. Any good general purpose plant food, such as a 10-10-10 (10% nitrogen, 10% phosphorus, 10% potassium), will correct the deficiency.

The specific fertilizer you choose will include directions for use, but as a general guide, 4 tablespoons of a 10-10-10 fertilizer per 4- to 6-foot shrub is plenty.

Fertilizers specifically for "acid-lovers", such as gardenia, camellia, leucothoe, and skimmia, may be needed if you live where both soil and water are naturally alkaline.

Mulching

A mulch is a layer of material applied on top of soil to cover and protect it. It is an efficient way to keep soil cool and conserve moisture. Mulches help prevent weeds and soil compaction, and give a finished appearance to plantings.

Organic mulches, such as fir bark, sawdust, pine needles, and compost also improve soil as they decompose. Any type of organic material that does not compress and exclude air is a possible mulch.

Most mulches are best applied about 2 inches deep. You will need seven to eight 2-cubic-foot bags to cover 100 square feet to a 2-inch depth.

Pruning

Prune evergreen shrubs to maintain their good health and appearance, to promote or enhance their flowering, and to stimulate their rejuvenation. Some evergreen shrubs require regular pruning, others need very little. Special pruning demands of different shrubs are noted in the individual plant entries.

Every shrub, regardless of how much other pruning it requires, should have any dead or broken branches removed each spring. These are unattractive, block light from new growth, and invite pest infestation. Two branches that rub against each other also require attention. Remove the branch most out of place, or both, if necessary.

Tools: One-handed pruning shears, scissor or anvil cut, are most useful. Depending upon wood hardness, they can cut branches up to 3/4 inch in diameter. Use lopping shears or a small handsaw for larger branches. Use two-handed hedge clippers only for formal-shaped shrubs. You will need all these tools when rejuvenating older shrubs.

Watering

Drip watering systems are efficient since they apply water directly over roots at a rate soil can absorb.

A basin of firmed soil directs water to roots—however periodic repair is required.

Many types of sprinkler heads are available for your garden hose and are easy to move where needed.

Mulching

Bark mulch is available in many sizes. Uniform-size particles give plantings a neat appearance.

Irregular particles of low-cost shredded bark bind together to form a mulch that holds well on slopes.

Rock mulch does not wash away and lasts indefinitely, but does not add humus to soil.

Fertilizing

Spray leaves with foliar fertilizer for fastest results.

Time-release fertilizer pellets provide required nutrients for one to five years, depending on the manufacturer. Follow package instructions.

Granular fertilizer applied on surface promotes good growth. Use as instructed on package.

PRUNING CONIFERS

Needled evergreens require routine pruning each year to maintain their size and shape, to promote dense growth, and to repair winter damage.

Symmetrical growth: Some evergreens, such as pine, spruce, and fir, make a major growth push once a year, in spring. New growth is produced in long, symmetrical shoots known as "candles". Snapping off or cutting candles back one-half to two-thirds their length before needles enlarge, will encourage denser growth.

If a whole branch on a pine, spruce, or fir has to be removed because of disease or injury, cut it back to where it joins the trunk; likewise, cut off side branches where they join a main branch. These shrubs do not have dormant growth buds along woody branches. A stubbed branch will remain bare and gradually die.

Random growth: Evergreens, such as juniper, yew, and hemlock, grow slowly and steadily throughout the growing season, rather than in a short spurt. Prune them anytime from spring to midsummer, as needed. Avoid pruning in fall—pruning stimulates new growth that might not mature and harden before winter. Also, fall pruning leaves bare stubs that will remain obvious and unattractive all winter. Since the shrubs grow slowly, try to hide wounds by cutting inside the shrub where branches join.

Conifers that have random growth can be sheared with two-handed hedge clippers. This creates a formal-looking plant with square or rounded contours. Shearing promotes a dense outer layer of foliage, but leaves the inside of the shrub bare.

For a more natural and informal look, prune with a one-handed pruning tool. Reach inside the shrub and cut out selected long branches, taking care to maintain the natural shape of the shrub. This thins the interior of the plant and promotes thick foliage. Shorten the tips of the remaining branches. Pruning in this manner controls the size of the shrub without destroying its natural outlines.

PRUNING BROAD-LEAVED EVERGREENS

Broad-leaved evergreens with small leaves, such as Japanese holly, boxwood, privet, and euonymous, can be sheared or pruned in the manner described for random-growing conifers. Large-leaved kinds must have selected branches thinned and shortened. Be sure not to cut through the foliage of coarse-leaved shrubs, as this will result in a ragged look.

Unless otherwise noted in the encyclopedia, prune broad-leaved shrubs after the shrub's flowering cycle is complete. Even if you grow a shrub for its berries and not its flowers—hollies or cotoneaster for instance—remember that berries develop from flowers. Prune these shrubs as necessary, perhaps a little after flowering and a little in fall and winter.

PRUNING HEDGES

The types of plants used for hedges can tolerate heavy shearing so begin shaping your hedge right away. Plants used for informal hedges—such as cotoneaster—are pruned, not sheared. To lessen their density, remove larger, interior branches. To make an informal hedge more dense, pinch tips of new growth.

Formal hedges require frequent shaping with hedge shears. If you have a lot of hedge pruning, consider investing in electric hedge shears. When using electric shears, keep in mind that it is very easy to inadvertently cut a power cord—or a hand. Also, if you slip-up with electric shears, you can seriously damage the plant.

Proper taper is the most important aspect of formal hedge pruning. The hedge base must always be wider than the top. If not, lower branches are shaded and gradually die.

Problems and Solutions

Some evergreen shrubs are prone to attack by insect pests such as aphids, caterpillars, leaf miner, scale, spider mites, and whiteflies. Bacterial or fungus diseases can also infect their branches, roots, or leaves. If a plant species is frequently plagued by any of these problems, that information is included in the plant listings. You will also find a column in the care charts on pages 60 to 62 that indicates whether or not an evergreen shrub is considered pest-resistant. By using this information when selecting plants, you can help keep your garden problem-free.

Insect pests and diseases can be controlled chemically, physically, or biologically. In recent years the trend has been away from chemical spraying in favor of physical controls—such as hosing pests off—and biological controls—encouraging useful insects such as ladybugs and lacewings to stay in your garden. In a book of this size it is impossible to recommend a treatment program for every potential insect pest or disease. The effectiveness of control measures will vary, depending on the season, region, and the type of weather when treatment is administered.

Good maintenance procedures, and regular close observation of the plants in your garden can help minimize problems. Early detection and prompt treatment for insect pests and diseases that may occur make control easier, and usually will help keep the problem from becoming devastating.

If you spot symptoms of disease or pest infestation, such as brown or spotted leaves, dead branches, dying flower shoots, unusual growths, or cracked, oozing bark, cut off a small portion of the infected plant and show it to your nurseryman, who can usually identify the problem and recommend an effective treatment program.

Another good source of information on plant pests and diseases is your County Agricultural or Extension Agent.

Pruning

A hedge with a wide top (left) loses lower branches from shading. If correctly pruned branches remain (right).

For an informal shape, thin branches at their origins with a hand clipper. Results in looser, more open growth.

For a formal shape, shear off outer growth with two-handed hedge shears. Results in dense foliage.

Clip back random-growing needled evergreens once or twice during spring or summer to control size.

To control size and encourage dense growth, clip or pinch back candles of pines when they enlarge in spring.

Pinch back growth of broad-leaved evergreens in spring to control size and promote denser branching.

Problems and Solutions

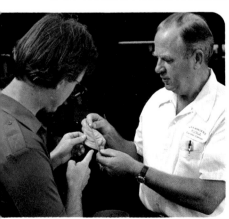

Take advantage of the gardening expertise available at your local garden center.

Chlorosis retards plant growth. It is characterized by yellowing of foliage between leaf veins.

To correct a chlorotic condition, spray foliage with a fertilizer containing chelated iron. Follow package directions.

59

Planting and Care of Evergreen Shrubs

This chart shows in easy-to-use form the basic information about planting requirements and follow-up care for each of the top-rated evergreen shrubs discussed in this book. It is a quick reference guide to help you determine what conditions and care a particular shrub needs to grow successfully. More detailed information on planting and care of particular plants is given in the encyclopedia entries.

PLANT NAME	Exposure			Water			Soil					Fertilizer			Pruning			Pest Resistant
	Sun	Partial Shade	Shade	Plenty	Regular	Drought Tolerant	Acid	Alkaline	Well-drained	Fertile	Infertile	Heavy	Regular	Light	Heading	Thinning	Season	
Abelia x grandiflora	■	■			■		■	■	■	■			■	■	■[1]	■	early spring	yes
Baccharis pilularis	■				■	■	■	■	■	■	■			■		■	late spring	yes
Berberis sp.	■	■		■	■	■	■	■	■	■			■	■	■[1]	■	early spring	yes
Buxus sp.	■	■	■	■	■		■	■	■				■		■[1]	■	early spring	yes
Callistemon sp.	■				■	■	■	■	■	■	■		■	■	■[2]	■[3]	early spring	yes
Camellia sp.	■	■	■	■	■		■		■			■	■		■[2]	■[3]	after flowering	no
Carissa grandiflora	■			■	■		■	■	■	■			■	■	■[2]	■	early spring	yes
Ceanothus sp.	■				■	■	■	■	■					■		■	after flowering	no
Chamaecyparis obtusa	■				■		■		■	■			■		■		early spring	yes
Chamaecyparis pisifera	■				■		■		■	■			■		■		early spring	yes
Cistus x purpureus	■				■	■	■	■	■	■	■			■	■	■	after flowering	yes
Cleyera japonica		■	■	■	■		■		■			■	■			■	after flowering	no
Cocculus laurifolius	■	■	■	■			■		■				■		■[2]	■[3]	spring	yes
Convolvulus cneorum	■				■	■	■	■	■					■		■	spring	yes
Coprosma repens	■	■			■	■	■	■	■	■	■		■	■	■[2]	■[3]	spring	yes
Cotoneaster buxifolius	■	■			■	■	■	■	■	■	■	■	■	■	■[1]	■	after flowering	no
Cotoneaster congestus	■	■			■	■	■	■	■	■	■			■		■	after flowering	no
Cotoneaster dammeri	■	■			■	■	■	■	■	■			■	■		■	after flowering	no
Cotoneaster lacteus	■	■			■	■	■	■	■	■	■		■	■	■[2]	■[3]	after flowering	no
Dodonaea viscosa	■			■	■	■	■	■	■	■	■		■	■	■[2]	■[3]	spring	yes

[1] — Takes shearing; [2] — Informal hedge; [3] — Espalier; [4] — Pinch new growth;
[5] — Afternoon shade inland; [6] — Pinch candles; [7] — Slightly; [8] — Cool climates; [9] — Hot climates

PLANT NAME	Exposure			Water			Soil					Fertilizer			Pruning			Pest Resistant
	Sun	Partial Shade	Shade	Plenty	Regular	Drought Tolerant	Acid	Alkaline	Well-drained	Fertile	Infertile	Heavy	Regular	Light	Heading	Thinning	Season	
Elaeagnus pungens	■				■	■	■[7]	■[7]	■	■			■	■	■[1]	■[3]	spring	yes
Escallonia x exoniensis	■	■[9]		■	■	■	■	■	■	■			■		■[1]	■[3]	after flowering	yes
Euonymus fortunei	■	■	■		■		■	■	■	■			■	■	■[1]	■	spring	no
Euonymus japonica	■	■		■	■		■	■	■	■	■			■	■[1]	■	spring	no
Euonymus kiautschovica 'Manhattan'	■			■	■		■	■	■	■	■			■	■[1]	■	spring	no
Fatsia japonica		■	■	■[9]	■		■	■	■			■	■		■[4]	■	spring	no
Gardenia jasminoides	■[8]	■	■	■	■		■		■	■		■	■		■[2]	■[3]	after flowering	no
Grevillea 'Noell'	■				■	■	■	■	■	■	■		■	■	■[2]	■	after flowering	yes
Hebe sp.	■[8]	■[9]		■	■		■	■	■	■			■		■[2]	■	after flowering	yes
Hibiscus rosa-sinensis	■	■[5]		■	■		■	■	■	■		■	■		■[2]	■[3]	after flowering	no
Ilex x altaclarensis 'Wilsonii'	■	■	■	■	■		■	■	■	■			■	■	■[1]	■[3]	early spring	no
Ilex aquifolium	■	■[9]		■	■		■		■	■			■		■	■	early spring	no
Ilex cornuta	■	■			■		■	■	■	■			■		■	■	early spring	no
Ilex crenata	■	■	■		■		■		■	■			■		■	■	early spring	no
Ilex vomitoria	■	■			■		■	■	■	■			■		■[1]	■	early spring	no
Juniperus sp.	■				■	■	■	■	■	■	■		■	■	■[1]	■	spring	yes
Leucothoe axillaris	■[8]	■	■	■	■		■[7]		■	■			■			■	spring	yes
Leucothoe fontanesiana		■	■	■	■		■		■	■			■			■	spring	yes
Ligustrum japonicum	■	■			■	■	■	■	■	■			■	■	■[1]	■	any time	yes
Ligustrum lucidum	■	■		■		■	■	■	■	■	■		■	■	■[1]	■	any time	yes
Mahonia sp.	■[8]	■	■[9]	■	■		■	■[7]	■				■	■	■	■	early spring	no
Murraya paniculata		■		■	■		■	■	■	■		■	■		■[1]	■	spring	yes
Myoporum laetum 'Carsonii'	■				■		■	■	■	■	■		■	■	■[2]	■	spring	yes
Myrtus communis	■	■	■	■	■		■	■	■	■			■	■	■[1]	■	spring	yes
Nandina domestica	■	■	■	■	■		■		■	■			■	■		■	early spring	yes

[1] — Takes shearing; [2] — Informal hedge; [3] — Espalier; [4] — Pinch new growth;
[5] — Afternoon shade inland; [6] — Pinch candles; [7] — Slightly; [8] — Cool climates; [9] — Hot climates

PLANT NAME	Exposure			Water			Soil					Fertilizer			Pruning			Pest Resistant
	Sun	Partial Shade	Shade	Plenty	Regular	Drought Tolerant	Acid	Alkaline	Well-drained	Fertile	Infertile	Heavy	Regular	Light	Heading	Thinning	Season	
Nerium oleander	■				■	■	■	■	■	■	■		■	■	■[2]	■	after flowering	no
Osmanthus heterophyllus	■	■			■	■	■	■	■	■			■		■[1]	■	spring	yes
Photinia x fraseri	■	■			■		■		■	■			■		■[2]		after flowering	yes
Picea sp.	■				■		■	■	■	■	■		■	■		■	spring	yes
Pieris sp.		■		■	■		■		■	■			■			■	remove spent flowers	yes
Pinus sp.	■				■		■	■	■		■		■	■	■[6]	■	spring	yes
Pittosporum tobira	■	■			■	■	■		■	■			■	■	■[2]	■	after flowering	no
Platycladus orientalis	■	■			■		■	■	■	■				■	■		early spring	no
Prunus caroliniana	■	■			■		■	■	■	■			■		■[2]	■	spring	yes
Prunus laurocerasus	■	■[9]			■	■	■	■	■	■			■		■[2]	■	after flowering	no
Pyracantha sp.	■				■	■		■	■	■	■		■	■	■[2]	■[3]	early spring	no
Raphiolepis indica	■	■		■	■	■	■	■	■	■				■	■[2]	■	after flowering	yes
Rhododendron hybrids		■		■			■		■	■		■	■			■	after flowering	yes
Rosmarinus officinalis	■				■	■	■	■	■	■	■		■	■	■[2]	■	after flowering	yes
Sarcococca hookerana humilis		■	■	■	■		■		■	■			■			■	after flowering	yes
Skimmia japonica		■	■	■	■		■		■	■			■			■	after flowering	no
Taxus baccata	■	■	■		■		■[7]	■[7]	■	■			■		■[1]		early spring	yes
Taxus cuspidata	■	■			■	■	■[7]	■[7]	■	■			■		■[1]		early spring	yes
Taxus x media	■	■			■	■	■[7]	■[7]	■	■			■		■[1]		early spring	yes
Thuja occidentalis	■	■		■	■		■	■	■	■		■	■	■	■		early spring	yes
Tsuga canadensis 'Pendula'	■	■[9]		■	■		■		■	■		■	■			■	early spring	yes
Viburnum odoratissimum	■	■[5]			■		■	■	■	■			■		■[2]	■	spring	yes
Viburnum suspensum	■	■[5]			■		■		■	■			■		■[2]	■	spring	yes
Viburnum tinus	■	■[5]			■		■	■	■	■			■		■[1]	■	spring	yes
Xylosma congestum	■	■		■	■	■	■	■	■	■	■	■	■	■	■[2]	■	early spring	yes

[1] — Takes shearing; [2] — Informal hedge; [3] — Espalier; [4] — Pinch new growth;
[5] — Afternoon shade inland; [6] — Pinch candles; [7] — Slightly; [8] — Cool climates; [9] — Hot climates

Name Cross-Reference

A plant can have many common names but has only one proper botanical name. The following list matches common names with their botanical names. The parts of a botanical name are the *genus, species,* and *cultivar* (or variety). The genus name signifies the general group to which the plant belongs, and together with the species name describes a particular plant. The cultivar is the name between quotation marks. An "x" between the genus and the species indicates the plant is a hybrid, formed either naturally or by breeders.

Common Name	Botanical Name
Abelia, Glossy	*Abelia x grandiflora*
Andromeda	*Pieris sp.*
Andromeda, Mountain	*Pieris floribunda*
Aralia, Japanese	*Fatsia japonica*
Arborvitae, American	*Thuja occidentalis*
Arborvitae, Eastern	*Thuja occidentalis*
Arborvitae, Oriental	*Platycladus orientalis*
Azalea	*Rhododendron* hybrids
Barberry	*Berberis sp.*
Barberry, Mentor	*Berberis x mentorensis*
Barberry, William Penn	*Berberis x gladwynensis* 'William Penn'
Barberry, Wintergreen	*Berberis julianae*
Bottlebrush	*Callistemon sp.*
Bottlebrush, Lemon	*Callistemon citrinus*
Bottlebrush, Weeping	*Callistemon viminalis*
Box	*Buxus sp.*
Boxwood	*Buxus sp.*
Boxwood, Common	*Buxus sempervirens*
Boxwood, Littleleaf	*Buxus microphylla*
Bush Morning-Glory	*Convolvulus cneorum*
Camellia, Japanese	*Camellia japonica*
Camellia, Sasanqua	*Camellia sasanqua*
Cherry Laurel, Carolina	*Prunus caroliniana*
Cleyera, Japanese	*Cleyera japonica*
Cocculus, Laurel-Leaf	*Cocculus laurifolius*
Cotoneaster	*Cotoneaster sp.*
Cotoneaster, Bearberry	*Cotoneaster dammeri*
Cotoneaster, Dwarf Silver-Leaf	*Cotoneaster buxifolius*
Cotoneaster, Pyrenees	*Cotoneaster congestus*
Cotoneaster, Red Clusterberry	*Cotoneaster lacteus*
Coyote Brush	*Baccharis pilularis*
Cypress, False	*Chamaecyparis sp.*
Cypress, Hinoki False	*Chamaecyparis obtusa*
Cypress, Sawara False	*Chamaecyparis pisifera*
Escallonia	*Escallonia x exoniensis*
Euonymus, Evergreen	*Euonymus japonica*
Euonymus, Spreading	*Euonymus kiautschovica* 'Manhattan'
Fetterbush	*Leucothoe sp., Pieris floribunda*
Firethorn	*Pyracantha sp.*
Firethorn, Formosa	*Pyracantha koidzumii*
Firethorn, Narrowleaf	*Pyracantha angustifolia*
Firethorn, Scarlet	*Pyracantha coccinea*
Firethorn, Tiny Tim	*Pyracantha* 'Tiny Tim'
Flowering Fruit	*Prunus sp.*
Gardenia	*Gardenia jasminoides*
Grevillea, Noell	*Grevillea* 'Noell'
Heavenly Bamboo	*Nandina domestica*
Hebe	*Hebe sp.*
Hemlock, Sargent Weeping	*Tsuga canadensis* 'Pendula'
Hibiscus, Chinese	*Hibiscus rosa-sinensis*
Hibiscus, Tropical	*Hibiscus rosa-sinensis*
Holly	*Ilex sp.*
Holly, Chinese	*Ilex cornuta*
Holly, Christmas	*Ilex aquifolium*
Holly, English	*Ilex aquifolium*
Holly, Japanese	*Ilex crenata*
Holly, Wilson	*Ilex x altaclarensis* 'Wilsonii'
Holly-Grape, Chinese	*Mahonia lomariifolia*
Holly Olive	*Osmanthus heterophyllus*

Common Name	Botanical Name
Hopbush, Hopseed Bush	*Dodonaea viscosa*
Indian Hawthorn	*Raphiolepis indica*
Juniper	*Juniperus sp.*
Juniper, Chinese	*Juniperus chinensis*
Juniper, Creeping	*Juniperus horizontalis*
Juniper, Savin	*Juniperus sabina*
Juniper, Shore	*Juniperus conferta*
Laurel, English	*Prunus laurocerasus*
Laurel-Leaf Cocculus	*Cocculus laurifolius*
Laurel-Leaf Snailseed	*Cocculus laurifolius*
Laurustinus	*Viburnum tinus*
Leucothoe	*Leucothoe sp.*
Leucothoe, Coast	*Leucothoe axillaris*
Leucothoe, Drooping	*Leucothoe fontanesiana*
Lilac, California	*Ceanothus sp.*
Lilac, Wild	*Ceanothus sp.*
Lily-of-the-Valley Shrub	*Pieris japonica*
Mahonia	*Mahonia sp.*
Mahonia, Leatherleaf	*Mahonia bealei*
Mirror Plant	*Coprosma repens*
Mock Orange	*Pittosporum tobira*
Morning-Glory, Bush	*Convolvulus cneorum*
Myoporum	*Myoporum laetum* 'Carsonii'
Myrtle, True	*Myrtus communis*
Natal Plum	*Carissa grandiflora*
Oleander	*Nerium oleander*
Orange Jessamine	*Murraya paniculata*
Orchid-Spot Rock Rose	*Cistus x purpureus*
Oregon Grape	*Mahonia aquifolium*
Photinia, Red-Tip	*Photinia x fraseri*
Pieris	*Pieris sp.*
Pieris, Japanese	*Pieris japonica*
Pine	*Pinus sp.*
Pine, Dwarf Scotch	*Pinus sylvestris* 'Nana'
Pine, Dwarf White	*Pinus strobus* 'Nana'
Pine, Mugo	*Pinus mugo*
Privet	*Ligustrum sp.*
Privet, Glossy	*Ligustrum lucidum*
Privet, Japanese	*Ligustrum japonicum*
Prunus	*Prunus sp.*
Rhododendron	*Rhododendron* hybrids
Rosemary	*Rosmarinus officinalis*
Silverberry	*Elaeagnus pungens*
Skimmia, Japanese	*Skimmia japonica*
Snailseed, Laurel-Leaf	*Cocculus laurifolius*
Spruce	*Picea sp.*
Spruce, Alberta	*Picea glauca albertiana*
Spruce, Norway	*Picea abies*
Sweet Box	*Sarcococca hookerana humilis*
Taupata	*Coprosma repens*
Tobira	*Pittosporum tobira*
Viburnum, Laurustinus	*Viburnum tinus*
Viburnum, Sandankwa	*Viburnum suspensum*
Viburnum, Sweet	*Viburnum odoratissimum*
Wintercreeper	*Euonymus fortunei*
Xylosma, Shiny	*Xylosma congestum*
Yaupon	*Ilex vomitoria*
Yew	*Taxus sp.*
Yew, English	*Taxus baccata*
Yew, Hybrid	*Taxus x media*
Yew, Japanese	*Taxus cuspidata*

Index

Main plant listings indicated by bold numbers.